T0130205

A COMPREHENSIVE GUIDE TO

GETTING HIRED
TEACHING

Achieve Your Ideal Teaching Position

A COMPREHENSIVE GUIDE TO

GETTING HIRED
TEACHING

Achieve Your Ideal Teaching Position

CARLOS HELENO

A COMPREHENSIVE GUIDE TO GETTING HIRED TEACHING
ACHIEVE YOUR IDEAL TEACHING POSITION

iUniverse books may be ordered through booksellers or by contacting:

iUniverse
1663 Liberty Drive
Bloomington, IN 47403
www.iuniverse.com
1-800-Authors (1-800-288-4677)

Because of the dynamic nature of the Internet, any web addresses or links contained in this book may have changed since publication and may no longer be valid. The views expressed in this work are solely those of the author and do not necessarily reflect the views of the publisher, and the publisher hereby disclaims any responsibility for them.

Any people depicted in stock imagery provided by Thinkstock are models, and such images are being used for illustrative purposes only.
Certain stock imagery © Thinkstock.

ISBN: 978-1-5320-1347-8 (sc)
ISBN: 978-1-5320-1348-5 (e)

Library of Congress Control Number: 2016921363

Print information available on the last page.

iUniverse rev. date: 03/10/2017

For Sara, Katherine, and Madeline

"Great teachers and great teaching transform lives, yet little is written on the career paths of prospective teachers and how they go about securing employment at the schools and institutions where they would like to make a difference. Winning candidates stand out from the rest in terms of their values and skills. Above all, they have worked on themselves. *Getting Hired Teaching* provides the perfect handbook for personal and professional development to ensure you become the best person for the job, and provides timely information on current trends in education, hiring practices and interview techniques. Written in a clear but compassionate style, this great book will help you make a flying start as an educator, or move your career up to the next level."

Tom Butler-Bowdon, author of the 50 Classics series, including *50 Psychology Classics, 50 Self-Help Classics, 50 Philosophy Classics*

www.Butler-Bowdon.com

Contents

Detailed Contents

Preface

This book is born out of the urging of colleagues whom I've worked with over the years in a variety of administrative capacities. Having read hundreds of résumés and cover letters, spoken with multitudes of teacher candidates, and interviewed hosts of promising educators, I've seen what works effectively in teacher profiles and watched how promising candidates in interviews transform into effective teachers in the classroom.

As well, many times in my career, I've been asked to help friends and colleagues write personal statements, résumés, and cover letters or provide guidance on effective interview strategies. It's from these various experiences and urgings that this book has come about.

In these past twenty years as an educator, leading young adults on service projects to developing countries, teaching a variety of grade levels and subjects in two prominent independent schools, working closely with athletes in cocurricular activities, and serving on a variety of leadership committees, I've come to learn that what appeals to me most about schools is the personal connection: the interactions between educators, between teachers and students, and between faculty and parents. Above all, it is witnessing students striving to achieve and then succeeding. For me, education—both teaching and learning—is about building relationships and developing rapport with students, with parents, and with faculty.

There is no doubt that great teaching and great teachers have a significant impact on students and their long-term association with school and with learning. Thirty years have passed since my high school days, but I'm continually reminded of the influence one particular teacher had on me and, inevitably, my career as an educator.

I think, at its core, this is the purpose of this book.

If we can recognize what makes us unique and how we can positively impact our students, then we can make teaching much more meaningful and learning much more rewarding—essentially, a transformative experience for our students. Effective learning and effective teaching feed each other, and it's my hope that through this deliberate approach we will be successful as educators.

But first, we need to get hired teaching.

Carlos Heleno

Introduction

What does it take to get a job teaching? What are school administrators looking for in a new hire? What are the best skills to have? Where do we even begin? We all struggle with these questions when we first start tackling the job search.

The purpose of this book is to prepare you for a successful application process so that you secure a teaching position in the grades, the subjects, and the schools you desire. Attaining a professional job may seem daunting when you first begin the search, but with preparation, focus, and determination, you'll achieve your goal.

The three most important messages to keep in mind as you go through this process are as follows:

- You are a unique individual whose upbringing, educational background, and life experiences have given you distinct values, beliefs, attitudes, and skills.
- You can become the effective educator you want to be and live a fulfilling life teaching students the subjects and grades you desire.
- You can position yourself well and achieve that teaching job through the right presentation and promotion of your talents.

The Problem

The teaching profession seems saturated with many new college graduates waiting to get into full-time positions in school districts for which there are so few openings. With the increase in concurrent teaching programs at universities, the appeal of the profession, and the success of the retirement plans, there appears to be an abundance of teachers in the marketplace and a scarcity of jobs available.

Because the supply of teachers is so high and the demand so low, we're looking at a surplus of professionals out of work in their particular field of expertise having to take part-time jobs in unrelated industries, volunteer for years in teaching-related fields, or be out of work entirely as they await openings in schools. Just as real estate is all about location, so too is education. Families move into neighborhoods with good schools, and good schools draw great teachers. The more desired a place is to live, the greater the increase in great schools and great teachers, and the reduced availability of teaching positions.

School administrators—and schools, by extension—are benefitting enormously from this saturation of the marketplace because they have many highly qualified professionals seeking these very few desired positions. They get to choose from the best of the vast applicant pool. For schools, this is a blessing; for teachers, well ... not quite the same.

Administrators sort through the myriad applicants for that one key person who stands apart from the crowd and seems to be the unique individual who can truly serve the school community.

And the applicant pool *is* vast.

Consider this: How many teachers graduated from the same college program in which you were enrolled? How many now have full-time teaching positions? How many are on waiting lists that are one, two, or even five years in length? Compound that with the many more teacher college programs available throughout the country along with the multitude of teachers who've finished programs in prior years, and the total number is staggering.

The Solution

In order to secure a teaching position, a candidate *must* stand out from the rest. For you, this means effectively strategizing your application process and positioning yourself as the most desirable applicant or, better, the *only* applicant to be considered. By leveraging your core values and core skills in a way that makes you an exceptional candidate and by uniquely marketing and boldly promoting yourself, school administrators have little choice but to acknowledge you and consider your candidacy. The message? Create a compelling vision of *you* as an outstanding educator, and recruiters will notice.

This is the focus of this book.

The Need for This Book

Technological innovation is having a significant impact on the job-application process. The traditional practice of applying directly to the employer using a cover letter and a résumé isn't exclusively practiced by each institution. Most schools and school districts require electronic copies of documents uploaded to databases, at which point applicant-tracking systems filter for predetermined criteria. The benefits of programs and services like these are indisputable: applicants with well-written cover letters and résumés containing key words are the first captured.

Developing persuasive cover letters and résumés is critical to securing a teaching position. Those *selected* as the best from the pool of applicants are those who have met all the criteria for which the software filters. Knowing what criteria schools are looking for requires close investigation as well as a planned approach to include these in the relevant documents.

In addition, writing a compelling personal statement and a detailed teaching philosophy achieves multiple objectives, including identifying your goals, your reasons for becoming an educator, your beliefs about teaching and learning, and what you have to offer the prospective school. Completing these primary steps helps you to infuse your cover letter and résumé with rich terminology and to present your professional persona in an appealing manner, one that will invariably capture the employer's attention.

You may never be asked for a personal statement or a teaching philosophy from a potential employer, but that doesn't discount their importance. You are after a job, and that means doing what it takes to get hired. Personal statements and teaching philosophies get you that much closer.

From this original pool of applicants, candidates are shortlisted. Administrators have their chance to peruse these teacher profiles. Within fifteen to thirty seconds, the average administrator has glanced over the documents and selected even further. At this point, a very short list of applicants sits before her. If you have prepared effectively, she will spend more time reading your résumé and cover letter. The more time she spends studying your résumé and reading your cover letter, the more your name, your credentials, your experiences, and your achievements stand out. The process is simple, but the results are finite. You hold her attention and move her from seeing you as a virtual character on paper to a compelling person with substance and potential as a professional educator in her school.

What is your online presence like? If someone were to search your name, what would he find?

Your social media profile is increasingly more significant in determining your candidacy for a job as it more candidly depicts who you are than the professionally written résumé or cover letter do. After all, these documents are highly polished and crafted devices while online postings, photos, and blogs are typically frank and honest expressions of the real person. School administrators would be negligent if they did not complete a thorough investigation of your social media presence. With so much career-deciding material available online, administrators must judge whether a candidate is the proper *fit* for the school. Is the person a good role model for students? Does the candidate demonstrate the values and skills of a teacher-professional? Is there any material online that could be deemed questionable and influence children and students in ways unfitting with the school's mission?

Social media now serves as an extension of the candidate's application and increasingly acts as the predominant determiner of an applicant's success—the résumé and cover letter are *hardly* the exclusive sources human resource personnel consult. Even reference letters are not enough in today's technology-rich society. Leveraging social media effectively to help you in the application process is a necessary strategy. The traditional application forms of résumés and cover letters will be around for a long time. Coupling them with the more current modern-day forms—including LinkedIn—will not only improve the quality of your application but also increase your chances of securing the position you desire.

Standing out in the crowd of teachers in order to be recognized by school administrators is your most important task. Knowing who you are and skillfully marketing yourself is the solution to achieving your dream job.

So … what makes you unique? Why would a school hire you? What do you have that a thousand other teachers don't?

Let's find out.

Chapter Overviews

Chapter 1 explores the current trends in the field of education from three distinct perspectives: the forces driving change in education, how these forces require teachers to address the needs of twenty-first-century students, and what it takes to be an exceptional educator. Trends in teaching have always existed, but with the recent democratization of learning and the exponential growth of technology and social media, they have increased significantly. Understanding these forces and their impact on the various constituents within a school community enables you to be better prepared for the job-application process.

Chapter 2 focuses on the current hiring practices within schools and school districts. Practices vary from one institution to another, and human resource personnel use a wide variety of criteria when evaluating new hires. Given that there is such a broad range of expectations for new teachers and that there is such a variety in what school administrators are looking for in candidates, it is important to have a comprehensive range of all expectations. This puts you in the most desirable position for hire.

Chapter 3 provides an overview of the proven tactics for acquiring jobs. Strategizing the application process is essential for success, and following a step-by-step process ensures that all points have been covered, increasing the likelihood of success.

Chapter 4 asks one simple question: who are you? Through a series of activities, you will explore your work habits, attitudes, behaviors, and skills all in an effort to determine your core values and core competencies. Defining your personal and professional personas helps you to focus your intents. Recognizing how your interests and talents align with the teaching profession confirms your skill set and prepares you for the next stage of developing your teacher profile.

Chapter 5 explores the roles of the significant documents in the application process: professional goals, personal statements, teaching philosophies, résumés, and cover letters. Techniques for building comprehensive and persuasive documents along with Top Ten lists for writing each complement these chapters. Impressive candidates have impressive documents, and being impressive isn't as difficult as it may appear. Leveraging your talents, crafting your profile, and presenting your personal best positions you for success in the application process.

Chapter 6 is all about effective techniques in preparing for the interview. From appearance, behavior, and mannerisms to best practices in responses, this chapter details methods for mastering the interview.

Chapter 7 guides you through each type of interview and offers a thorough overview of the process. Each stage is significant. The more you are aware of the nuances of each stage, the more effectively you can prepare for a successful interview.

Chapter 8 is the climactic step in this whole process, providing a comprehensive approach to the teacher interview and filled with dozens of practice questions and strategies. Documents and webpages all help to build the professional persona, but these only help to get you an interview. This final critical step will ultimately decide whether you get the job or not. No application process preparation is complete without the practice of an interview.

Who This Book Is For
This book is designed for various people:

Students: If you are currently completing an undergraduate degree or teacher college certification program, then you will find all the forms you need to design an outstanding teacher profile.

Teachers: If you are currently teaching and want to make a change from a particular grade or subject to another, or move to a different school altogether, then you will find all of the steps necessary to hone your efforts and prepare for the interview.

Educational professionals: If you are a professional in the field of education holding a complementary position but want to become a full-time educator, then you will find this comprehensive list of strategies invaluable.

Professionals: If you are currently in an entirely separate profession outside of teaching and looking to become an educator, then you will find a rich array of information highlighting the more poignant aspects of the teaching profession as well as all the necessary steps to consider in order to make a successful career change.

How to Use This Book

This book is designed in a step-by-step format in order to facilitate your preparation for the application and interview process.

First of all, you will learn many of the expectations employers have of their teachers. You will discover the values and competencies top schools and school districts find most significant. You will recognize and determine your own personal values and competencies and align these with the schools and school districts you deem to be the right fit for you.

Secondly, by completing each step in the order provided, you will develop the documents needed for submission, ensuring they are designed with the particular employer in mind and articulated in a professional manner, as well as with a keen attention to current educational practices and trends.

Thirdly, each step is designed to introduce you to the questions employers ask in the interview. Completing each genuinely and thoroughly will help you develop your responses to the top questions employers ask.

Consideration

The field of education is a rich and rewarding profession that holds many opportunities for you to challenge yourself to achieve great things for you and for your students. The job-application process, on the other hand, can appear to be a tedious as well as frustrating activity. But take it in stride. You have your whole career ahead of you. Focus on one task at a time, build on your successes, and soon enough, you will have great momentum leading you to the finish line. And then, you are a teacher.

A Note on the Text

Throughout this work, I have used the term "essential questions" coined by Grant Wiggins and Jay McTighe in their pivotal texts *Understanding by Design* and *Essential Questions* as a way of introducing thought-provoking concepts. These essential questions will stimulate your thinking and direct your planning as you pursue the application and interview stages of the job search.

PART 1

The Education Landscape

CHAPTER 1

Current Trends

Purpose

Preparing effectively for the application process requires an understanding of the current trends in the field of education. Recognizing the forces that impact education in the way students learn, teachers teach, and schools work gives you an advantage in the job search. As well, knowing what makes great schools, great school leadership, and great teaching sets you up for success, and this you can leverage to your advantage.

Essential Questions

- What forces are impacting the field of education?
- How are these forces changing the way students learn and behave?
- How do they change the learning environment?
- What are the current trends in educational theory?
- How are these trends impacting the way teachers teach?
- What are the new expectations for teachers?

The Modern Field of Education

Population trends, technological advances, and changing learning platforms are having massive implications for education as well as changing the traditional institutions of learning into dynamic centers of growth. The classroom environment is shifting quickly, unsettling established practices and introducing new models and approaches to effective teaching and learning. This is an era of innovation in which, increasingly, students are at the center of their own education with the potential to design their own learning in a unique and personalized way.

Social media and communications technology have impacted the way students participate in the classroom: what they learn, how they demonstrate this learning, what they produce, and how they produce it is substantially different from what it was in the past couple of generations.

Teaching and learning will only continue to follow this trend. Consider just these few forces: population growth; technological innovation; advancements in medicine; understanding of brain function; the rise of developing countries; the growing concern for health and wellness; the increased attention to marginalized people and communities; and the need for social, political, and global awareness and activism.

These forces impact our roles as educators. We see this in our increased need to address multiple learning styles; appeal to many cultural backgrounds; engage English language learners; keep abreast of brain research; ensure that each student is living a healthy and active lifestyle; draw the outside world into the classroom or take students into the outdoor classroom; and increase exposure to the natural world, to culture, to history, and to service.

With so much going on, now is the time in which the field of education asks for teachers to be both broad in their experiences and specialized in their chosen disciplines.

An effective educator who can embrace the ever-changing teaching and learning environment, maintain resilience and strength under this pressure, dynamically participate in the development of new practices, and continue to foster a love of learning stands a greater chance of captivating students and appealing to their needs. Invariably, this person will have a great impact on her students, giving them the best possible opportunity for growth and development, for building character, and for success in the twenty-first century.

Effective educators are understanding and accepting of change. They know that teaching and learning are constantly evolving. They have a desire to do what is best for the students and continue to implement new theories, adopt new strategies, and put *best practices* into practice.

They embrace innovation. They deepen their understanding and broaden their skill set.

Effective educators are capable of profoundly shaping the future of their students with their global awareness, sense of humanity, and desire to see everyone successful in all that they do.

Does this sound like you? Do these statements inspire you to become a better teacher? The teaching profession is waiting for you, looking for you, and may not know where or how to find you.

How will administrators know who you are and what you are capable of achieving? How do you capture their attention? How do you convince them you are the one to hire? How do you market yourself?

In the coming chapters, we will answer all of these questions. They are not that difficult. In fact, you have most of the answers already. All we need to do is focus efforts, and the answers will begin to come to light.

The New Student

Exceptional educators have introduced us to many concepts of human growth and development. Some focus on emotional intelligence, learning styles, and brain development, while others look at how technological and socioeconomic forces change the teaching landscape. Comparing what students need today to what they needed just twenty years ago produces a stark difference. Looking forward into the future and considering what students will need in another twenty years will reveal an overwhelmingly different scenario, one hardly fathomable. How will the Internet—which continues to evolve—impact learning? How will software and hardware change schools? How will social media revolutionize the way we communicate? The way we behave? The way we respond? What can we expect of artificial intelligence? What other technologies are yet to be introduced? What other great forces will impact teaching and learning? If it is true that undergraduate programs are introducing students in first year to concepts that will become obsolete by the time they graduate, then what is in store for education? What is in store for educators?

No doubt, you have spent time learning about these forces, collaborating with your peers, and even anticipating what is to come. Keeping abreast of the current trends is critical to being an effective educator and—in this case—marketing yourself as a relevant teacher of this technological age.

How is your knowledge of twenty-first-century skills? How do you ensure you are appealing to the needs of students so that they can become productive members of society? How do you lead them to build strength of character? How do you develop them to find balance and happiness in what they do?

Reviewing prominent leaders in the field of education gives us a broader perspective on the changing nature of the teaching and learning landscape. While there are many great educators, for our purposes, exploring three major thought leaders gives us a wide enough scope of the salient topics. In particular, Tony Wagner highlights the skills necessary for success in this century, Ken Robinson offers guidance on finding one's place in this world, and Martin Seligman explores the importance of personal fulfillment in life. Each of these in some way tackles issues teachers should be aware of.

Tony Wagner

From a very economic perspective, Tony Wagner sums up the essential capacities for the twenty-first-century student in seven distinct skills necessary for success. His works—specifically *The Global Achievement Gap* and *Creating Innovators*—challenge us to consider the problems of our current education systems and the need to address those skills that will lead students to succeed as they face the changing socioeconomic climate of our world. Consider these:

1. Critical thinking and problem solving
2. Collaboration across networks and leading by influence
3. Agility and adaptability
4. Initiative and entrepreneurship
5. Accessing and analyzing information
6. Effective oral and written communication
7. Curiosity and imagination (Wagner 2008)

As educators, we understand that every subject we teach in every grade level has many objectives that lead to mastery. While we want to meet each of these and ensure our students develop the requisite knowledge and skill set, we also have to look to these seven general skills from a much broader perspective and consider them as part of our curriculum. We cannot deny any one of these skills as unnecessary in our modern culture.

How do we ensure we are meeting these skills? How do we develop a curriculum that addresses each? How do we know this curriculum is effective? What activities lead to honing them?

Tony Wagner's work is invaluable to teachers. From an administrative perspective, it is expected that you are aware of it and addressing it in your classroom. It also serves as a road map for becoming an effective educator. You will find it captivating, enlightening, and a validation of who you are as a learner.

Sir Ken Robinson

In Sir Ken Robinson's works—*The Element* and *Finding Your Element*— he drives home the point that schools need to change. If students are not turned on to school, then there is something wrong with the system. Teachers need to make connections with students. They need to learn what their interests and talents are and help them develop these. Only in this way do students stand a chance of enjoying school, making the most of it, and finding a career suitable for them. Robinson explores the importance of finding your place in life—your passion, your element. But he does so by including a host of examples in people who found success *despite* their educational upbringing: Paul McCartney with music, Matt Groening with art, Gillian Lynne with dance—each who did not find inspiration in school.

Why read these works? We need to find new ways of appealing to students. Despite all the curriculum expectations, an overarching goal of education is to help students discover their personal talents and lead them to finding meaning in what they do.

This can appear challenging for teachers when there is so much to get done in any given day. But effective educators make personal connections with students. The get to know them. They recognize their talents. They direct them. They support them. And they celebrate their successes. Applying a one-size-fits-all industrialist approach to education is tantamount to ignoring the individual needs of each student and watching raw potential wither away from lack of nourishing.

Robinson reminds us that every student is worth our time and effort, and his works are worth reading again and again. Through his recognition of the talented personalities and their experiences with education, we are reminded of our responsibilities as educators. We are not simply teaching a series of expectations; we are helping to craft a child. What we do in the classroom and how we do it will have tremendous repercussions on our students.

How do we apply Robinson's teachings in our own practice? How do we discover student talent? What methods of instruction result in students finding *their* element? How do we ensure that we are not simply reflecting our own bias on students but helping them discover who they are?

If you haven't yet seen it, watch Sir Ken Robinson's TED Talk "Do Schools Kill Creativity," which at the time of this writing is still the most popular video with more than forty million views.

Martin Seligman

Another great educator from the positive psychology movement is Martin Seligman. He provides a road map for successful achievement and fulfillment in life. In *Flourish*, he offers the PERMA model—a strategy for bringing about well-being and happiness. People who focus on positive emotions, engage in meaningful tasks, develop positive relationships with others, and who look for opportunities to constantly accomplish or achieve goals live a much happier and more fulfilled life. They find meaning in what they do and, invariably, contribute to society in a meaningful way.

For Seligman, authentic happiness and fulfillment are the ultimate goals. With the great attention now paid to mental wellness and the growing concern for long-term health, his research is timely and necessary for educators. Seligman's concern for mental health is a boon for teachers who have students with a host of learning styles coming from a diversity of socioeconomic conditions and a variety of family dynamics. As well, the increasing complexity of society, the pervasive role of social media, and the ubiquitous nature of technology further compound the circumstances.

Seligman speaks of the need to build resilience and character in order to navigate the many forces of change around them. Maybe the best way to ensure students have a chance to live a successful and happy life is to guide them to put things into perspective, build coping strategies for difficult times, and develop ways of approaching life's circumstances with a positive outlook. As educators, we can see the importance of teaching students to become happy, fulfilled, and contributing members of society who have concerns for themselves, for each other, and for the world around them.

So, how do we ensure we are developing students of character who are resilient, focused, and morally guided? How do we teach so that students find value and fulfillment in what they do? How do we engender the importance of positive emotions and relationships?

Other Great Educators

There are a host of other educators and topics that can be explored thoroughly, including Howard Gardner's works on multiple intelligences; Carol Dweck's exploration of the success mind-set; Daniel Goleman's study of emotional intelligence; Barbara Coloroso's books on valuing the independence of children; and Robert Marzano's application of brain research on classroom practice. Couple these contemporary writers with the more traditional authors of significance in educational literature and you have a thorough study of this dynamic field. Any one work yields a wealth of valuable insight that informs our practice. Deliberately understanding and applying these theories results in an improved performance in us as educators and in our students as learners.

Our sense of the *new student* will continue to change with increased research and increased application of theory into practice. Meeting all of the needs of students is like attempting to hit a moving target; after all, change happens so quickly we are often managing the results of influences rather than anticipating and planning for them. Nevertheless, it is an important exercise. Being an educator, being a professional who cares about his students' successes requires this constant practice of trial and error. And while this may have always been the case for educators, it has become a greater priority with the current forces of change.

For us, in the process of finding a teaching position, understanding modern educational theory, reading some of the more influential texts on a variety of disciplines, studying great educators, and absorbing and applying these theories and strategies in our own practice makes us much more desirable candidates.

Increased Expectations of Educators

Sometimes referred to as a calling, sometimes a vocation, teaching can hardly be termed a job. Undeniably, it is a complex process with many variables that require careful attention. Consider just this handful. Teachers are skilled in their target subject matter, in addressing the needs of the students, in creating the optimal learning environment, in continuing to build relationships with all stakeholders, and in maintaining an understanding of current trends in education. They personalize instruction, guide students to optimal performance, and celebrate their successes. Teaching takes enormous effort, focus, and dedication. Great teachers strive for excellence in themselves and their students as well as a positive and lasting learning experience for all.

Just as educators strive for this level of excellence, so too do administrators for their new hires.

School administrators are looking for *outstanding*. They are looking for highly dedicated professionals who do what is right by the student and the school, who raise the school's standards, and who raise student performance levels. They are looking for these professionals to contribute to the greater school community, to give additional time to cocurricular activities, and to provide service where needed. Administrators are looking for professionals who are exceptional in conduct, personable in nature, and a pleasure to have around. The list of expectations is vast. In essence, school administrators are looking for that unique person who will champion the mission and vision for the school, practice what is best in education, and continue to hone and master his or her craft.

Great schools are made up of great people, including students, parents, faculty, employees, and all others who are in any way associated with the school community. School leaders do not want to hire just anyone.

They want the best. They want great teachers who will add to the culture of the school and make it stronger and more appealing. They want outstanding educators because these people will draw in better students and better teachers and increase the reputation of the school.

For the person looking to get hired, this means that you must *be* outstanding.

And you are.

So how do you present yourself as that outstanding educator?

Below are overviews of the many expectations administrators have of new teacher candidates. Consider the essential questions as warm-ups or primers to the fuller discussions to come.

1. Meeting Standards

Standards are significant. Principals need to ensure their schools meet standards set out by governments. But they are also out to exceed these. It's not enough to achieve just the minimum, and often, principals have their own benchmarks. There is pride in a school that is very successful. People want to be a part of something great, and a school recognized for achieving high standards raises its profile. Parents want to send their children there, and faculty flock there.

But also, schools like to distinguish themselves from each other. Sometimes this means adopting more rigorous and challenging world-class curriculum. Enrichment programs like Montessori, Advanced Placement, or International Baccalaureate all have their own set of standards, and these greatly exceed the government's. Religious schools or culturally centered schools equally have their own mandates.

School leaders are going to look for greatness in their prospective candidates and wonder whether they have what it takes to meet standards and even exceed them.

Essential Question: How do I ensure I am not only meeting standards but also enriching my programming and delivering a world-class education?

2. Addressing Student Needs

Today's classrooms contain a broad range of learners showcasing a variety of abilities and coming from multiple socioeconomic backgrounds. Any class might contain English language learners, children of single-parent households, and culturally diverse students. The composition of the class necessitates remediation for some and enrichment for others.

From a broader perspective, modeling values and building character education into daily interactions with students seems paramount. Educators motivate and inspire students to learn and find meaning in tasks. They also cheerlead and celebrate student successes.

But these are still pretty general in scope.

Personalizing education is about making a connection with each student, learning what motivates him or her, and developing strategies to appeal to him or her in particular. Identifying the learner's academic history and building a plan based on the individual needs of the student are important steps. Adjusting the plan given the progress both the student and teacher make is an added pressure in addressing student needs.

Essential Question: How do I ensure I am appealing to individual student needs and giving each student the best opportunity to learn, grow, and find fulfillment in what they do?

3. Employing Multiple Teaching Strategies

Teachers need to master many techniques to appeal to various learning styles and ability levels. Addressing student needs means creating an inviting and dynamic environment where students can feel comfortable in taking risks with their learning. Meaningful lessons and units not only teach the theory but also provide practical application in ways that are accessible to students.

Technology and social media serve a host of purposes. Leveraged effectively, they hold great promise for improving learning. Teachers who leverage these effectively and innovate approaches to student engagement gain an advantage and further personalize the learning experience for students. But if these only serve to entertain, then they are used in futile ways.

Teaching is as much about content knowledge as it is about engaging students, innovating delivery, strategizing methodologies, and making learning worthwhile.

Essential Question: How do I effectively employ proven strategies to enhance the learning experience for students but also continue to innovate in my delivery of curriculum?

4. Building Community

Too often, media depicts teachers as autocrats isolated in their own classrooms and masters of that finite space with no connection to the real world—and maybe this is simply a product of what many of us witnessed growing up in our schools, real or not.

But this isn't what teaching really is like. Educators are integral members of the greater school community. They work closely with their colleagues, engage parents in their child's development, and consult with educational specialists. Building rapport and developing trust with all community members is the sign of a healthy and vibrant learning space. When we embrace the community, students are excited to be in our classes, parents feel comfortable in contacting us, colleagues are encouraged to work closely with us, and administrators feel welcome in our classrooms.

Essential Question: How do I build rapport and develop trust with students and parents such that they value and appreciate me for who I am and what I can offer in creating a meaningful learning experience?

5. Practicing Professionalism

Educators are professionals. They have had the formal training in undergraduate degrees and then in postgraduate programs. They are certified by a college with specific standards of practice, and there is an expectation from the greater community that they exhibit the character traits of professionals.

As with other professions in the care of children, standards for educators are high both in practice and ethical behavior. In fulfilling a capacity of authority, there is a significant power differential with students in a vulnerable position looking to teachers for guidance, care, and direction.

Standards of professional practice include being progressive and keeping current with educational trends, being a reflective practitioner and applying new learning, and being a change agent and leading, managing, and contributing to learning communities. Teachers are moral, ethical, and diplomatic. And they are proficient in communication with students, colleagues, and parents.

Essential Question: How do I develop and maintain a level of professionalism of an exceptional educator?

6. Managing the Classroom

Things are managed, and students are *led*.

Managing the classroom is often understood to mean maintaining order, keeping students motivated and engaged in a productive task, and respecting each other and the learning environment. Order, process, protocol, and rules are great management systems that work effectively in a classroom.

Discipline often falls under this heading as well. There are consequences for not abiding by the rules, and students seem to learn best when they know the boundaries. Breaking rules results in punishment and—if the discipline is effective—curbed behavior.

Well-managed classrooms, where systems are in place, allow teachers to focus on leading students through their learning rather than spending an exorbitant amount of time on consequences to poor behavior.

Developing as a teacher-leader improves practice. An autocrat or strict disciplinarian is going to be less effective as an educator in a school setting that calls for much more personalized education. The cost to the classroom environment is taxing and to the teacher, detrimental; after all, how often does a "Who's the boss?" confrontation end with everyone's dignity intact? Lee Canter's *Assertive Discipline* strategies for classroom management and Barbara Coloroso's *kids are worth it!* for raising children with dignity are great reads. Applying a few of their strategies improves effectiveness in the classroom.

Essential Question: How do I ensure I maintain a respectful classroom environment where the focus is on learning and engagement and not on rules and consequences?

7. Keeping Organized

A portion of time in a typical day is dedicated to keeping organized. This includes a broad range of tasks, such as maintaining thorough and detailed lessons, coordinating the submission of all assignments, managing notebooks and textbooks, recording anecdotal comments, reporting on student achievement, and organizing and managing multiple tasks simultaneously. An effective teacher needs to be detail oriented.

A teacher's ability to keep many tasks going simultaneously is directly proportional to her success as an educator. The more competent she is at managing all of the minutiae, the more effective she is in her delivery, and the more positive the learning experience. Students sense competence and confidence. Although they may not be able to articulate it in words, their actions and reactions communicate clearly whether the teacher is proficient in his practice or not.

Great teachers develop systems for every aspect of their teaching. Systems maintain order and structure and provide clarity and focus. Students learn best when they can rely on an orderly process.

Essential Question: What systems can I put in place for a smooth running of my classroom?

8. Leading Others

Teachers are leaders. They lead in the classroom, they lead each other in the school, and they lead in the community. Recognizing that teachers play a significant role in setting standards of behavior, attitude, and values goes a long way in understanding the full impact a teacher has on the school community.

Ask many adults who the most significant people were in their lives, and a better part of the responses will indicate teachers. It is difficult to deny this. After all, teachers are there from preschool through university entrance. North Americans are typically in school through till their twenties, spending the majority of their day on school or school-related activities. If we extend the notion of teaching beyond the classroom to coaching a team, leading a club, or running a band, the breadth of ways teachers influence students increases dramatically. Educators are everywhere. It's not just subject matter they teach. It is participation, leadership, responsibility, discipline, cooperation, independence, and many, many more life skills.

How teachers lead impacts how students learn. And what teachers do in the classroom permeates through the school community.

Essential Question: How do I lead as a teacher?

9. Communicating Effectively

Much of education is about communication. It must be clear and deliberate. Without clarity, students are confused, frustrated, and at a loss. Whether it is communicating lessons orally, recording feedback on assessments, or sending out newsletters, e-mails, or blog postings, every medium requires competence in its composition. The form and the function dictate the style. A more casual oral delivery may not be called for in the more formal realm of e-mail. Effective communication results in confidence and trust in the messenger.

Educators are held to a higher standard of communication. It is expected that teachers have a greater level of competence given their education and by virtue of their role as leaders.

But effective communication isn't just about delivering; it is also about receiving. For teachers, listening is a vital aspect of communication. Listening to a student express his frustration at his inability to solve a problem is much more informative for us as educators in coming up with a strategy.

Essential Question: How do I develop effective communication strategies to improve my performance?

10. Providing Additional Attention

While addressing student needs may be about personalizing instruction, providing additional attention is all about offering more to students. Today's educators must be globally minded, proficient in the use of technology and social media, adept in cocurricular activities, and sensitive to service in the immediate school community and at large. This could manifest as coaching a team, running a club, or providing a service. It could mean becoming more involved with school community events and taking on initiatives not directly impacting students in the classroom.

Educators who cannot meet these expectations lose their power of influence and quickly become redundant. Keeping relevant is the key.

Essential Question: How do I continue to be relevant for students and for teaching and what can I do to keep myself in demand?

Next Steps

By the time students graduate from high school, they will have had between twenty and forty different teachers—each with his or her own style of teaching. Some will have been very effective. Some memorable. Others, neither.

What does it take to be an exceptional teacher?

Students have a great sense of what makes an exceptional educator. If a teacher can engage them, keep them motivated, set high expectations for them, allow them to stretch and learn, then he is an effective teacher. But even this is an incomplete list. Students are biased, after all. They may prefer one teacher over another because that teacher connects with them in a way that others do not.

How do we judge effectiveness in teaching and greatness in teachers?

In the coming chapters, we will explore what makes a great educator and look at ways of identifying those character traits within you that are effective for teaching. Recognizing these strengths, building on them, and enhancing your talents will increase your effectiveness and set you apart as a great educator.

Hiring Practices

Purpose

Having a general understanding of current hiring practices informs your job search process. If you know what school administrators are looking for in new hires, then you know how to market yourself. The better you understand the whole process, the better you can direct your next steps.

Essential Questions

- What are the current hiring practices?
- What are school administrators looking for in teacher candidates?
- Who do school administrators hire?
- What does it take to be an exceptional teacher?
- What are the expectations for teachers today?

Hiring Practices

Schools and school districts can vary significantly in their hiring practices. On one end of the spectrum are the institutions that have a highly formalized process, including a very strong human resource department and list of criteria sought for in a new hire. On the other end of the spectrum are schools whose hiring committees have no experience, do not know what they are looking for, and hardly have a proper list of criteria to follow. And there are many varying models in between.

Schools with best practices in hiring tend to follow a polished protocol. There is a process of determining need, defining the criteria of the teacher candidate, marketing the school, and advertising the position. There is a system for submission of documents and a series of steps to follow from initial application to final offering. It is a highly involved process taking many hours and multiple people—including human resource personnel, teachers, department heads, vice principals, principals, and various other administrators. This model is ideal for schools and school districts that need to manage hundreds of applications at a time. It is also ideal for the individual who wants consistency in protocol.

The other extreme has schools operating more organically based on need and hiring personnel—experienced or inexperienced. These schools can often function on intuition rather than a very tight protocol or set of criteria. This works well for the school, as it has so much more autonomy over the whole process. But for the individual, it could be a little more complicated because the uncertainty variable seems higher.

As you begin the application process with schools and school districts, you will discover a variety of practices. Keeping detailed notes on each school's expectations for submission of documents will prove beneficial in the long run as you can quickly become mired by the variety of methods. Are you directing your application to the school in an e-mail? Who is receiving the message? Is it a principal or an administrator? Are you uploading your application to a general database that multiple schools will access? Which schools will have access? Being vigilant here reduces your level of confusion and helps you focus your efforts on marketing yourself.

Later on, we will look at the specific criteria to include in your application so that you are ready for any process followed. But first, I would like to share a common experience I have at recruiters' fairs. While this anecdote sheds a bit of light on the variety of teaching opportunities available, it is more about the mind-set of the candidate.

Recruiters' Fairs—A Personal Anecdote

Over the past dozen years or so, I have had the opportunity to meet with thousands of new faculty at recruiters' fairs. Like an amusement park, the doors open at ten in the morning, and in a large room, dozens of tables are lined with programs and brochures and tall banners bordering them. At any one of these events, five hundred to seven hundred college students who are soon-to-be teachers walk through the doors eagerly anticipating meeting the person who will offer them a job. They come dressed professionally, loaded with résumés and cover letters, sometimes doling out business cards. They are armed with many questions about job prospects and ready to be interviewed on the spot.

A variety of educational institutions are represented at these trade shows, including local school districts, independent boards, coalitions of schools, private organizations, oversees schools, tutoring agencies, and even experiential education companies. This rich assortment holds a lot of promise for aspiring educators who arrive to find a candy store filled with dozens of flavors. Eagerly, they rush to their favorite tables to speak with human resource personnel, school representatives, school districts, company owners, or whoever is operating the booth.

School districts are the first visited. The school representatives smile and are courteous as they share the details of the application process. Unfailingly, they have nothing to offer and explain how waiting lists for permanent positions number in the years. A little discouraged—but not surprised—the new faculty move to other booths and hear messages from a host of other independent organizations, less favored but still promising. Certainly a little more encouraged, they engage in discussions about the possibilities present at private schools or denominational coalitions. They even consider the opportunities of travelling to foreign countries to teach English and get a world experience.

By about one thirty, much of the room is cleared of students, and the place resembles an abandoned circus with some booths entirely taken down, others in midprocess as banners are wrapped up and programs put away, and what is left is an eerie feeling as the whirlwind of activity dies down to nothing.

Throughout this three- to four-hour event, I watch hundreds of new faculty enter the room, move about, at times in a frenzy, at times in a calm, collected state. There are many mixed emotions: anticipation, excitement, confusion, uncertainty, and even discouragement. Repeatedly, they hear *we're not hiring now* and walk away wondering what they will be doing for the next few years.

Others take full advantage of the opportunities present. They hear many promising things about the possibilities of teaching at particular schools—job postings, professional development opportunities, travel, small class sizes, benefits—and their feelings change from discouraged to encouraged.

When new faculty come to our booth, we give glowing feedback about our schools and share opportunities and experiences that we have had or that our colleagues have had. We continue to encourage looking beyond school districts—which tend to be magnets for new teachers. There are many positions available if people are willing to look for them and take the time to understand them. There are thousands and thousands of private and independent schools that are always hiring. These positions can be highly rewarding and offer a different teaching experience to the standard school district model. There are many opportunities to teach abroad, which can be very lucrative in nature, allow someone to build confidence through practice, and then, once ready, return as an experienced educator—something all schools are looking for. There are a host of tutoring agencies available, which give teachers a chance to refine one-on-one skills with students.

When we share anecdotes with new faculty and speak of the benefits an alternative educational institution offers, we get a very different response. At first, there is skepticism and fear, mostly because teachers are not well informed of these non-school-district schools. Others are highly encouraged and turned on to the possibility that they just might get hired soon if they focus on alternate opportunities.

I am always excited at the prospects available, and having served in two first-rate independent schools and held half a dozen administrative positions, I see the opportunities available that others may not, and I continue to advise people to look widely and broadly because they may just find the perfect place to teach that they would not have known about otherwise.

My message to these faculty, as it is in this book, is to remain positive and optimistic about the potential, stay focused on the goal, persist in your efforts, and be confident that you will achieve.

To new faculty, it must be overwhelming. Everyone around them has a teaching certificate, and everyone is competing for a scarcity of teaching positions—or so it appears. But this mentality is limiting and can debilitate a person's momentum and effort. Among the many questions new faculty ask, there is one overriding message I always like to share. We are all talented in different ways and have had a multitude of unique experiences. In order to position ourselves best for a teaching job, we must leverage these experiences and talents in a way that differentiates us as well as enhances the school.

What makes you unique? Ask yourself this question again and again. If you are applying to a school district for which there are few if any positions, how do you stand out from others? What do you have to offer that differs from them? To use business terminology, what is your *unique selling proposition*? Take this a step further and add, how can this unique selling proposition *enhance the school*?

Who School Administrators Hire

Administrators are looking for *exceptional* educators.

Among the hundreds or even thousands of applicants, there are a breadth of educational backgrounds, teaching experiences, and personality traits. Finding those unique people who are best suited for the teaching position available is a challenge. The school is looking for a particular type of educator, and from their perspective, there are many diamonds in the rough. How does a school proceed?

It is obvious that the criteria for a grade-six homeroom teacher differs significantly from a grade-twelve physics teacher. But why should the criteria for a senior kindergarten teacher in one school be very different from that of another school? Administrators do not always have a common list of criteria they work from. This could be because the school's vision or mission differs. It could be that the school culture needs an influx of vibrant new educators. It could also be that administrators are looking for people they work best with. In some cases, it could be that they really do not know what they are looking for and are using their colleagues' list of hand-me-down criteria and interview questions. There are so many reasons for the discrepancies.

Regardless, administrators are looking for the *best fit*. They have a unique school with all of its idiosyncrasies and want a match for that particular environment. Sometimes, schools are looking for a teacher to fill a short-term obligation, a long-term occasional, or simply a one-year contract. Sometimes, they are looking for permanent hires. What makes one teacher better than another? What gets one teacher hired and not another?

Exceptional educators stand the chance of fitting in in any circumstance. They have the character traits that lead them to success in multiple contexts. Exceptional educators are talented, diverse, flexible, and adaptable. They take on a challenge willingly and work at it until they succeed. They are open to feedback and take direction well. These kinds of teachers are always in demand. Whatever the educational background or previous experience, best practices suggest that the best educators are those who are teachable. Content and skill can always be learned by someone who is willing. Hiring the right people is the most important step for schools because teachers can then be trained in improving their effectiveness.

Top Ten Traits Administrators Are Looking for in a New Hire

In general, school administrators are looking for effective teachers, and effective teachers have many talents.

1. **Competency.** Knowing what to teach and how to teach is competence. Being resourceful and finding out what you do not know or how to better deliver a lesson is competence. People who do not know and cannot do are not effective educators.

2. **Versatility.** Someone who is versatile is knowledgeable about a host of subjects and has a broad skill set. This trait is in great demand because schools often have needs to be filled but might not have the necessary resources. For instance, hiring someone simply to teach one section of a course would be outrageously costly and counterintuitive. Teachers who are versatile, who possess a broad array of talents and experiences and can fill the need, are highly sought after.

3. **Flexibility.** Change is inevitable in the classroom. Despite the best efforts of teachers to plan appropriately for lessons, they must have the flexibility to change at a moment's notice to deal with the particular circumstance. Disruptive student behavior, malfunctioning hardware, and fire drills are common interruptions

that can mean changing initial lesson plans. Remaining flexible and able to shift gears when faced with these disruptions makes for a much smoother teaching and learning experience. Rigid behavior can lead to disappointment and frustration—emotions that do not suit the teacher professional.

4. **Adaptability.** As educational theory continues to improve and as forces impact the education system, adapting to change becomes increasingly more important. Sometimes this requires adopting new processes, learning new programs, or changing delivery methods. Sometimes this means taking on a subject you have never taught before, teaching a grade you are a little less comfortable with, or completing a project that causes you to step out of your comfort zone.

5. **Teachability.** Someone who is teachable does not have all the answers but is willing to consider alternate perspectives and wants to learn and grow and become a better educator. This is a highly sought after character trait.

6. **Patience.** Some concepts take moments to master; others, years. Teaching and learning require enormous patience. Students may learn through fits and spurts, showing great initiative but then fumbling or making mistakes in judgment that thwart their learning or growth. Patient educators support their students, recognizing that the learning continuum is slow and steady. Both students and teachers progress through these stages. For teachers, some lessons and units are exceptional; some flop. Mastering teaching is a long and involved process. Educators sensitive to the learning curve are effective.

7. **Caring.** Great teachers care about their students' well-being; they put the needs of their students high and advocate for them. They support them when they make mistakes, and they encourage them when they feel defeated.

8. **Confidence.** Students can sense a teacher's lack of confidence. They might not be able to articulate it, but they show it with their choice of words and behaviors. A confident teacher has greater control over his classroom, leading the students and managing the curriculum. The students are aware of the rules, the

boundaries, and the disciplinary actions; the teacher is prepared with his lessons, instructs appropriately, and gives prompt and competent feedback. When a teacher lacks confidence, it shows in these areas.

9. **Diplomacy.** Undoubtedly, there will be times when teachers need to deal with difficult circumstances: an angry parent, an unsupportive administrator, or an ineffective assistant. Education is about relationships. Building strong, respectful relationships with all constituents makes difficult experiences much easier to manage. As a new teacher, your reputation is established quite quickly—practically the first few days and weeks of the school year. Entering the profession with some conflict-resolution strategies and keeping in mind that the focus of education is to support students in their growth and development ensures everyone will be respectful of your decisions, whether or not they agree with them.

10. **Communication.** Effective communication appears in many forms, including kinesthetic, visual, and auditory. Teachers use eye contact, facial expressions, and body language; they speak clearly, articulately, patiently; they listen to their students with care and attention; and they write anecdotes, report card comments, newsletters, e-mails, and feedback on assessments. Communication says much about the communicator; effective communication results in improved learning.

Who Secures an Interview

The common practice schools follow in shortlisting candidates for interviews comprises multiple steps. At first, a human resource person or administrative assistant scans the many cover letters and résumés submitted by applicants and separates them into *yes* or *no* stacks. This tends to be the first level of filtration. Assistants then print off the electronic documents and highlight terms that are distinct, intriguing, and somehow suggest that this person is worthy of further investigation, as she seems to fit the criteria sought for in the new hire.

Depending on the school, the *yes* stack is further whittled down by grade teachers or department heads. Vice principals and principals might have a say as well. This shortlisting will happen multiple times before the interview committee sees the complete list of candidates.

It's not just credentials administrators are looking for. If candidates do not recognize the need to present themselves as professionally as possible in their documents, they run the risk of not even being considered. Poorly composed applications suggest a lack of preparation and extend to the credibility of the applicant. Will this person put in the same lack of effort into teaching? Will this person formalize lessons, care for the students, and present professionally? A cover letter and résumé serve as the *audition* for a part in the play. If the audition does not pass on paper, then proceeding further with a formal interview seems a waste of time and effort. Writing effective documents that capture the administrator's attention are a must—hence, the focus of the second part of this book. Candidates who make the cut not only have a professionally written résumé and cover letter—and this does not mean they have hired professionals to compose their documents—but also have some intriguing qualities or experiences that warrant further investigation. They have captured the attention of multiple people and deserve to move to the next level, the phone screening.

At this point, someone will have the task of calling the applicants for a brief interview. A series of questions for each candidate are drawn up. These are personalized and designed to determine whether an official interview is granted. Just because a candidate gets a call does not mean that she gets an interview. For example, consider the person who has hired a professional to compose the documents, but the screen call reveals her Spanish speaking ability is far too rudimentary for the grade-eight core Spanish position available. Or the person whose cover letter suggests he is a strong communicator, but the phone screening reveals he's not articulate enough to teach university entrance English. There are many examples like this that validate the use of an effective phone screening process.

In their shortlisting process, administrators also have to consider the current school culture. Do they need to hire experienced educators or recent college graduates? An optimal balance is often sought. Enriching a department with faculty who possess a range of teaching experiences and credentials makes for a much stronger teaching team. Hiring faculty with years of experience adds credibility, foundation, and depth to the program, while recent graduates bring on new methodologies and change a potentially stagnant environment. Combining highly experienced teachers with tried and tested methodologies along with vibrant young faculty eager to try new things gives a school culture a dynamism that balances both tradition and change.

What I Look for in an Applicant's Profile

I consider the following characteristics to be the *gold standard* for a new hire. If she meets all of the criteria, then she is an excellent candidate and worthy of an offer.

- progressive educator
- innovative practitioner
- caring and nurturing character
- competence in subject matter
- depth of educational experience
- commitment to excellence
- moral and ethical behavior
- sociable and friendly personality
- diplomatic with parents, administrators, and colleagues
- supportive of school decisions
- willing to question policies and practices to improve programming
- resourceful and eager to implement best practices
- decisive in action
- effective manager of change
- breadth of teaching or practicum apparent
- ultimately, someone who is teachable

When I meet with prospective teachers or teachers looking to shift from one position or school to another, I look for these characteristics in their profiles. Some of the criteria I find pointed out explicitly. Some I find hinted at but not obvious enough. And some I do not see at all.

Achieving all of these criteria, however, isn't easy, especially for the new teacher. Nevertheless, the aim is important and the practice necessary. A candidate who exhibits these criteria may well be a candidate worth hiring—but so too is the candidate who strives to achieve these.

Young professionals sometimes come with these characteristics, having known for many years that they were destined to become educators. Everything they do reveals a natural inclination, a comfort level, and a confidence in teaching. These people need little guidance.

Many young professionals enter the field of education with a desire to become exceptional teachers but seek mentorship and need direction to help mold and shape them into teacher professionals. The desire is there, and so is the effort. These teacher candidates are in demand because they *are teachable*.

Criteria change from school to school and from administrator to administrator. What one is looking for, another is not. Knowing what one is looking for is hard to guess. Researching the individual school, studying the advertisement, viewing the website, speaking to other teachers, and taking a tour will provide a much more informed perspective.

If there is so much discrepancy between schools, how do you know what a hiring committee is looking for in a candidate?

My argument is simple. The above list comprises a broad spectrum of expectations, and meeting all of these puts you in the most promising position.

Sometimes schools are looking for more from their new hires. This could be because they are seeking experienced educators or teachers trained in a particular field of study. Consider the following additional criteria that schools seek:

- minimum teaching experience of five years
- experience in a language immersion program
- specialist education qualifications
- religious affiliation
- Montessori training
- varsity coaching experience
- Advanced Placement experience
- International Baccalaureate experience
- international travel experience

From the administrator's point of view, it is important to clarify to a job prospect which character traits a school is seeking. Some schools and school districts reveal very little and rely on the interviews heavily. Others post a minimum requirement before they will even shortlist for a screen calling. Detailed advertisements help. These outline criteria sought. But they do not reveal too much, just enough to suggest the kind of person they are looking for. Revealing too much information is like *teaching to the test*. If candidates know exactly what schools are looking for, they could cram for these, ace the interview, and get the job. But this does not make them genuine. What happens when the school year begins and the teacher realizes the persona he or she portrayed in the interview is not the real person holding that job? Either the teacher discovers her deception has resulted in getting a job for which she is not suited, or the administrators discover this—or worse yet, both. At this point, it will only become more problematic for the new hire who struggles in a position not fit for her, and the school struggles with how to handle this complicated situation.

Genuine character is synonymous with personal integrity.

On the other side of the table, when a candidate is hired, it is incumbent on the school to highlight those characteristics that captured the attention of the interviewing committee and on what grounds a decision was made to offer the position. After all, a teacher who knows why she was hired will have a greater understanding of what the committee was looking for. What stood out to them about her? Was it specific qualities, experiences, education?

Letting the new hire know serves a dual purpose. First, it is recognition of the candidate's talents and accomplishments—a pat on the back. People like to be recognized for what they are good at—it motivates and inspires them to continue performing. Secondly, it reinforces to the new hire what is expected of her in that school. It is as if the principal is saying to her, "This is why we hired you and what we would like to see you doing all the time." From the perspective of the school, spelling out for the candidate what the expectations are is an excellent tactic. Great schools have great induction programs, as they help new teachers transition to the profession and the school community. That transition happens at this moment following the interview.

Teachers who do not secure the position should consider calling the school and finding out why. This isn't in an effort to challenge the principal or human resources, as this would not lead anywhere anyway, but to learn from the whole application experience. How beneficial is it to you to learn directly from the people who interviewed you? If all you learn is that your responses to questions were vague or that you lacked confidence in your delivery, then this is very instructive to improving your interviewing skills.

In the many interviews that I have conducted, only once did a teacher call to ask for guidance and direction following a decision not to hire. She called to ask what we were looking for that she did not have. She also wanted to know how she interviewed and where she could improve. Providing feedback helped her understand herself as an educator and interviewer. She was thankful for the opportunity and no doubt found a position rather quickly thereafter given her resolve.

This is an admirable quality in a candidate but not always something manageable by a school or school district when hundreds of interviews are completed over a short period of time. Also, it is something administrators might hesitate to do in case they are held accountable for revealing a flaw or prejudice in their hiring practices—certainly a possibility. Nevertheless, consider it. You may just get a better sense of how you respond while in the hot seat. And then you can improve upon your delivery.

Achieving all of the criteria on this gold standard might seem a little too idealistic and impractical. After all, how many teachers do not have these same characteristics and yet have been effective educators and excellent role models, the best the profession has to offer? No doubt, there are many. But that's not what you are after. You are after a job, and that means being the best educator you can be so that you can get the job.

At times, many of the criteria are met, while some not at all. It becomes a judgment call at this point, and a decision is made that seems to be in the best interests of the school. Which criteria are administrators willing to forgo in a teacher candidate? Each person is different and has varying degrees of these qualities or characteristics, and making the right decision is a complicated process. For instance, an educator might have a host of great qualities, but his values do not align with the school's. For many administrators, this might mean the teacher does not make the final cut. If he does not have shared values, there may be difficult situations in the future when he will not be willing to get on board with a new initiative and instead stick stubbornly to his own practice.

Consider the supply and demand dilemma. If there are equally strong candidates given their experience, education, and diverse talents, then principals have the option of picking and choosing a candidate that meets certain criteria more. When the supply is high, there is choice for schools, and principals can make decisions easily.

Attracting, Training, and Retaining Talent

School administrators are charged with three tasks when it comes to hiring practices: attracting, training, and retaining talent. Attracting teachers is about finding the best among a host of highly qualified educators. Once hired, administrators train top talent to be effective. Retaining talent is about compensating talent. Teachers who are paid well, appreciated for their efforts, and given opportunities for growth and development, among many other criteria, stay on.

The application process is all about presenting yourself as the best possible teacher candidate you can be so that people take notice. If school administrators have done their best, then they too will have presented themselves in a way that makes you take notice. When both are aligned, a nice match is found.

As a prospective candidate, your task is all about the first of these three charges. When you are hired, the school will guide you through the transition and shape you into the educator that aligns with their vision and mission. Hiring is about finding teachers who are the right fit. The closer you are to being the right fit, the easier it is for the administrators to get you the rest of the way.

Next Steps

Knowing about current educational trends and hiring practices helps set the scene for you. The next big step is the job search. Where do you start? What is the best way to go about your search? How can you ensure you are directing your efforts well?

Effective processes produce successful results. You could spend a lot of time mired in all sorts of ineffective methods in hopes that something will work out. Or you could take a very deliberate and well-aimed approach to achieve your goal.

The next chapter is all about getting your strategy right so that your job search is effective.

The Job Search

Purpose

Given the current trends in education and the hiring practices of schools, the traditional job-application model requires an upgrade. The old methods of putting together a cover letter and résumé and waiting for a job posting before applying are not sufficient. This process might yield a job, but the chances are slim. Instead, it is important to modernize the whole application process so that the best job opportunities are made available to you. A deliberate and methodical approach to building your reputation and actively searching for ideal positions is required.

Essential Questions

- What is the best procedure for securing a teaching position?
- How do I ensure I have the requisite qualities school administrators want in a new hire?
- How do I position myself for a successful application process?

Strategizing Your Application Process

Securing a teaching position requires a resolute sense of purpose. You have to understand what it takes to become an outstanding educator and have an unwavering vision of yourself as that outstanding educator. Knowing who you are, what you want, and why you want it is clarity of thought. Then you must build an attractive profile and portfolio and market yourself to potential employers. You must have a determination to pursue multiple employment avenues and a relentless persistence to continue the search until you secure that teaching position.

Sounds impossible? Not really. When you think about it, getting a job entails getting to know yourself better, getting to know what you like doing and what you are good at doing, and then finding the right match for you in a school. The more you know each of these, the greater your chances of securing a job that brings you satisfaction and fulfillment. You don't *have* to know everything about yourself as you begin your teaching career—no one does. But you do have to be open to discovering who you are. You don't *have* to know everything about the school either. How could you until you were deeply entrenched in daily activities? But the closer you get to knowing each of these, the easier the transition and the greater likelihood of a successful placement.

Developing a plan that includes pursuing positions, researching schools, building your profile, marketing yourself, and strategically targeting teaching jobs is a recipe for success.

Identifying how you stand out from all the other teachers with similar qualifications and differentiating yourself further will help make you a more attractive candidate.

Search-and-Secure Process

Until you are hired, your job is *getting* a job. You won't be paid for it, but you will be investing in your future. It is easy to be blinded by lack and the feeling of hopelessness—but these don't get you anywhere. Teaching requires that you put in a minimum of eight hours a day and forty hours a week. Imagine how much you could accomplish in your job search if you put in eight hours a day and forty hours a week. You would put together an outstanding portfolio, and you would search for the best jobs, apply to many places, and practice the interview relentlessly. These strategies will get you the job.

Why take on a nonteaching-related position when it is going to take up all of your time? Sure you may have debts and bills to pay, but what are you after? Are you willing to sacrifice a little bit of time and money to achieve your goal? Because, if you are, it will not take long.

This is the purpose of the search-and-secure method. Settling for a job that might not fit your ideal school environment isn't going to get you what you want. Putting in the time and effort it takes will get you what you want. Focus, determination, and commitment to the pursuit of your goal will do it.

Here is how:

Search

- Search available teaching positions in school districts, organizations, agencies, and private and independent schools.
- Leverage teacher contacts, friends, and colleagues that may know of teaching positions available.
- Pursue teaching-related avenues in the meanwhile, including tutoring agencies, education workshops and seminars, education departments and consultants.

Research

- Develop a clear understanding of what school administrators are looking for in prospective candidates.
- Understand the school district or school's mission, vision, core values, core competencies, and strategic plan.
- Clarify the application process of that particular school or school district.
- Determine their hiring practices.
- Understand their expectations for teachers, the salary, and the benefits.
- Recognize teacher satisfaction, teacher attrition rates, and retirement rates.

Build

- Create a thorough profile of yourself as an outstanding educator.
- Design an exemplary portfolio of you as an educator.
- Develop a compelling reputation and personal brand.

Promote

- Market yourself to friends, colleagues, principals, and schools.
- Leverage your references.
- Leverage social media effectively in your personal campaign.

Target
- Customize your portfolio and profile, designing it uniquely for each school or school district.
- Relentlessly continue the search.
- Repeat the process until you've achieved your goal.

This tactical approach forces you to hone your efforts rather than blindly flinging arrows in all directions in hopes that one hits the mark.

What You Need to Do to Get Hired

If the marketplace is saturated with teachers looking for work, then you have to do what it takes to get the job. Do you have a list of your professional goals? Do you have a personal statement? Do you have a teaching philosophy? Do you have a personal brand?

No doubt, you have a résumé and cover letter. You probably also already have an idea of who you would ask to serve as references. But this is not enough. If you want to be outstanding in the sea of teachers, then you have to present yourself as outstanding.

A portfolio that includes a professional goals sheet, a personal statement, a teaching philosophy, as well as the résumé and cover letter appears much more impressive than a skeletal submission. Building an outstanding portfolio requires completing a few simple steps. In this chapter, we will look at these briefly. In the next, we will begin to build them.

Step 1 is all about your *professional goals*. Determining your short-term, intermediate-term, and long-term goals helps you clarify your plans and communicates a well-thought-out process to potential employers.

Step 2 is to develop your *personal statement*. This is a clear presentation of your core values, beliefs, and competencies in a persuasive passage. It is your opportunity to showcase yourself. Interviewing committees love to meet people who are self-assured. The better you know yourself, the easier it is to talk about yourself. And the more comfortable you are in talking about yourself, the more confidence you reveal. Confidence in who you are and what you offer reassures interviewing committees that you will approach teaching with the same level of conviction, and this is promising.

Step 3 involves sharing your *teaching philosophy*. Here is where your creativity manifests as you imagine your ideal classroom and present your beliefs and opinions about teaching, about learning, and about student success. Someone who understands what students need and knows how to appeal to those needs is a worthier candidate.

Step 4 entails putting this all into your *résumé*. When the interview panel scans the résumé and notices all of the keywords, the professionally organized and detailed thoughts, and the highly structured layout, it is difficult for them not to consider your candidacy seriously. Completing the first three steps makes for a well-crafted résumé.

Step 5 extends this process to your *cover letter*. Words of persuasion can reveal you as an exceptional candidate.

Step 6 is all about your *brand*. Leveraging social media in a way that complements your professional documents ensures you are presented to prospective interviewers as a professional educator worthy of a position at their school. Given how influential social media is in the hiring process, it is important to ensure your personal and professional personas align.

Step 7 requires securing professional support in the form of *reference letters*. Letters and references are instrumental to your success.

Step 8 is all about your *professional interview*. Having completed all the pertinent documents, you are more than prepared to begin practicing and mastering the professional interview.

Finding Jobs

It is always disheartening to hear that there is a *shortage of teaching positions* available and that *no one is hiring*. I often wonder how much of this message comes from a scarcity mentality, limiting beliefs, or media pushing the message. No doubt, there are many school districts that have long waiting lists. Teachers on these lists remain for long periods—sometimes years—completing long-term occasional positions or daily supply work in different schools until that waiting period is over and they finally secure a position. But this scenario is debilitating for someone eager to launch a career.

When I consider those who get trapped in this mind-set or who forgo entering the profession entirely because of this fear, I wonder if they have simply just narrowed their focus too much and eliminated many opportunities available. After all, there are many, many teaching positions out there. Schools are always hiring. Great educators are always in need.

I would like to paint a different picture altogether about job prospects, and hopefully, through this process, encourage you to broaden your options and consider opportunities beyond the norm.

Most aspiring teachers tend to think of landing a teaching position in their local school districts. They consider school districts the only places to work and their hometowns to be the only places to live. While I don't want to suggest that this vision is unattainable, I do want to suggest that there are many other options to consider. For instance, does it have to be a school district? What about a private school or an independent school? What about schools affiliated with a particular denomination or culture? What about schools fulfilling a particular teaching philosophy?

Of course, schools also come in a variety of forms. We tend to think of schools as yearlong with the following divisions: preschools, primary, junior, intermediate, and senior. But there are summer schools, crediting agencies, sports schools, colleges, and travelling schools. Have you heard of Class Afloat? Weeks at sea studying biology and taking Advanced Placement courses. Or what about Neuchatel, a finishing school in Switzerland where all students take only their grade-twelve courses? How about Global Journeys? Take four weeks. Travel Italy and the Mediterranean. Teach a grade-eleven or grade-twelve course. If you like travel, you will love these options.

There are also many opportunities to work in the teaching profession as a tutor while you are preparing for your dream job. How about working one-on-one with grade school children honing your teaching skills. Really digging deep into the craft. Listening to how students learn. Gauging their development. Helping them grasp knew concepts. Correcting their progress. Tutoring agencies are an exceptional way to become skilled at your craft because you get to see students learning close up. And you get to see which methods work best. Practicing different strategies for different students is essential to improving as a professional, and if you can do this before securing your job, then you will make transitioning to the role of teacher much smoother, let alone prepare for the interview more effectively.

Next Steps

The next step is to identify all of your values, attitudes, behaviors, habits, and skills by completing a series of reflective activities. Through this process, you will collect all of the keywords to use in writing all of your portfolio documents as well as prepare for an effective interview.

PART 2

You as a Professional Educator

CHAPTER 4

Who You Are

Purpose

The better you can identify your values, attitudes, work habits, and skills, the easier it is to compose your teacher portfolio and the more prepared you will be for the interview. Knowing your core values and core competencies makes the job search easier and helps you align yourself with the *right* school. Well-informed people have options and make the best choices; the ill informed run the risk of jeopardizing their job prospects.

Essential Questions

- What are your values?
- What are your attitudes and behaviors in regard to teaching and learning?
- How do you work?
- What are your skills?
- What makes you unique?
- How do you distinguish yourself from others?

Introduction

By this point, you have had a tremendous number of experiences. Your early home life, your schooling, your social interactions, and your jobs have all helped you make distinctions about who you are as well as helped you make judgments about what you like and dislike.

In order to put together a compelling professional portfolio, it is important to determine your strongest attributes, those qualities that define you as distinctly different from others. Differentiation is important. The more you can distinguish yourself, the more you stand out from the crowd. Having a rich personal profile puts you one step closer to securing that dream teaching job. The interviewing panel will undoubtedly have questions about who you are and what you intend to do with your life. Clear and carefully crafted responses will impress them and suggest to them that you are self-aware, organized, and prepared. Panelists like to see this. It promises that you will deliver this same level of care and attention to your work in the classroom.

Contrast a well-informed and well-spoken candidate with one who hesitates in the interview, struggling to think what her dominant personality traits are and then haphazardly identifying the first two or three terms that come to mind—despite their little relevance to her. Is the school even looking for a teacher with these qualities? Which would you hire if you were on the other side of the table?

Identifying your dominant personality traits is tantamount to excellent preparation for a successful application and interview. There are many great resources available to help in this process, including personality and psychological tests. For our purposes, the following activities are more than adequate as they will help you identify traits from four broad categories: your values, your work habits, your attitudes, and your skills. Each of these categories is relevant to your daily practice in the classroom. Identifying what you value, how you work, what your attitudes are to teaching and learning, and what your dominant skills are positions you for completing an accurate cover letter and résumé as well as prepares you for practically half of the interview.

Values

Why Values Matter

In a very basic sense, values are anything you give attention and effort to and can easily be determined by where you spend your time and money. You might value family and friendship or adventure and athletics. You might value respect and responsibility or cooperation and teamwork.

You might value faith and reverence or charity and piety. Each value is important and defines who you are. While you might change from time to time and adopt new values and discard the old, there are a few constant ones that continually direct your life and actions.

Recognizing your dominant values is paramount because values matter to your employers. If your values align with the school's, then you stand a greater chance of being hired. If not, there is little likelihood of a successful placement.

The Values That Matter Most

Great schools have great value systems. They post these in the halls and in their marketing paraphernalia and tout them at large gatherings. These are the *ideal* values schools strive to achieve every single day throughout the year during good times and when times are tough. They abide by them when they celebrate milestones and student successes. And they abide by them during the pressured moments before the report cards go out, the loss of a community member, or when a difficult decision needs to be made about a student or a faculty member.

Values drive decision making. A school that lives up to its values is a school to be admired and pursued as a great place to teach. The feeling is *just right* that great things are going on. Teachers, parents, and students are confident that the school is making the *best* decisions for all involved. There is no confusion or misunderstanding. *This* is a school worthy of *you*.

Great schools value their school community. Often, great schools have students, parents, alumni, faculty, employees, administrators, and board members all weigh in to help determine the core values. The process is time-consuming, strategic, and precise. What comes of these discussions isn't a simple collection of platitudes but a carefully thought-out and argued list of values.

These values are ingrained in the daily and yearly activities, the interactions between faculty and students and parents, and the way lessons are prepared, assessments taken, and successes celebrated. Values are a rich reflection of the history and culture of the school and are a testament to what the school intends in theory and performs in practice.

Knowing the school's values helps you determine whether it is the right fit for you. Working at a school whose values you do not support is counterproductive and may do you more harm in the long run than the good it does in the short term.

Consider this: How would you feel about working at a school whose top values include *zeal*, *wisdom*, and *reverence*? Would you be comfortable teaching at a school whose values are *faith*, *hope*, and *charity*? What about a school that places primary importance on *loyalty*, *honor*, and *sacrifice*? Which would you prefer? How do each of these values translate to your day-to-day teaching?

Schools tend to favor having three to five driving values. Among the top schools, a few appear repeatedly. Which values most align with your own?

Values of Top Schools

respect	compassion	hard work
responsibility	scholarship	kindness
integrity	balance	courage
honesty	community	strength
fairness	wisdom	will

One Caveat

Despite what may appear in their marketing, how a school operates on any given day or at any particular time in the school year may appear incongruous with the values established. It happens. No matter how idealistic a school's values, school leaders are going to do things at times that seem hypocritical, counterintuitive, or counterproductive. After all, people run schools, and people are prone to making decisions that sometimes do not seem to support the values the school endorses. The important thing to remember is that schools continue to aim for those values because as long as they continue to aim in the right direction, they have a greater chance of achieving the mark.

Your Core Values

Deliberately determining your core values pays dividends. Not taking the time to reflect on these could prove disadvantageous.

People can read body language and facial expressions at times better than they can hear words—especially human resource personnel who are better trained to look for signs. Interviewees can be saying one thing but meaning another, and this becomes apparent to the panelists. They might not be able to articulate this in words, and they might not be able to tell why or how, but they will know that something is *off* about the person's character. At some level, they have determined that what is said is misaligned with what they see.

Picture this: The debrief moment comes following an interview when the committee convenes to discuss all candidates. Statements like the following are tossed around: *I don't know. I expected more.* And, *she didn't present herself the way her résumé and cover letter suggested she would.*

Yes, that *is* what happens. Having interviewed many potential candidates over the years, the greatest waste of time was knowing that after only a few minutes it was abundantly clear that this person was not the right fit for the school, and then we had to continue through the next thirty minutes completing the interview. Why finish it, knowing that teaching at the school was no longer an option for the person? We believed in the need to respect the process, and this was an important first step for the teacher candidate. If we did not give that person our full attention and give him or her the opportunity to develop interviewing skills, then we would not be living up to our stated values.

Fortunately, determining your core values is easier than it appears. Just a few small steps and you come to terms with what you value most.

Interviewing committees like people who are clear about who they are, what they want, and how they are going to go about getting it. It makes the decision process easy for a committee. Either the candidate is obviously an option or he's not. No gray area. No second-guessing.

Determining Your Core Values

People tend to have a very good sense of their values. Some are easily identifiable. Other values, however, drive our thoughts and our behaviors but are not easily recognized until another person points them out to us.

A three-pronged approach to determining your core values ensures you have cast a wide-enough net to capture all of them.

The Personal Approach (Your Self-Analysis)
Consult the values table below. Check off any that describe you and add any that do not appear on the list. Consider prioritizing them by the amount of time you spend on each or by which are most meaningful to you. As you work through this list, think of your daily activities. What do you do on a day-to-day basis? Where do you spend your time? Which values most relate to your activities? Continue to rearrange the list, sending those of least importance to the bottom and those of most importance to the top. Determine to have a list of ten values ranked in order of greatest importance to least.

The Friends and Family Approach (Social Influencers in Your Life)
Leverage the power of family and friends by asking them to help you identify your core values. Survey them. Pole five people, and ask them what they would say are your top five values; after all, these people have a very good sense of who you are and what you are interested in.

Collate the lists. You will find that many of the same values keep coming up. But you may discover a few that you did not anticipate. Draw the repetitions to the top of the list.

There is this notion that you are the average of the five people you most spend time with. Take this notion a step further and reverse the survey. Evaluate the core values of the five people you most spend time with and average them out among the group. No doubt, the top few values you possess will closely align to those of family and friends who you are closest to.

The Professional Approach (Professional Influencers in Your Life)
There are many other influencers in our lives. Our professional circles, including work and school, are great places from which to capture values. Having your colleagues evaluate your core values can be very instructive, as you might find yourself presenting in a more formal and professional manner that differs from the more casual behavior around friends and family. Also consider looking to other people, including

teachers, coaches, and bosses, and other places like community centers, athletic teams, and religious institutions for further support.

Table 1: Values

balance	diversity	knowledge	scholarship
care	efficiency	loyalty	self-reliance
citizenship	enthusiasm	nurturing	service
collaboration	equity	optimism	strength
community	fairness	passion	teamwork
compassion	flexibility	politeness	transparency
competency	hard work	professionalism	trust
competition	helpfulness	progress	vibrancy
cooperation	honesty	reliability	vision
courage	independence	resourcefulness	will
creativity	innovation	respect	wisdom
dedication	integrity	responsibility	zeal
discipline	kindness	reverence	

Bringing It All Together

You now have three lists: one that you generated personally, one that reflects your more social nature, and one that more closely reflects your professional persona. How do these compare? Are they closely aligned? Are there values on others' lists that do not appear on your own? What values are ranked highest on these three lists?

Collate the lists and come up with a final top-ten list and transfer these to the "My Personal Profile" at the end of this chapter.

Values Reflection

What are your most dominant values? How aligned are your values with those of the top schools around the world? Would it benefit you to be at a school with perfect values alignment to your own? Or would you look to a school that you are not perfectly aligned with but that would offer you an opportunity to stretch and grow in that direction?

Attitudes and Behaviors

Your Attitudes and Behaviors

What are your attitudes toward teaching and learning? What are your behaviors around colleagues and administrators? What is your attitude toward change? How do you behave around parents of your students?

Your attitudes and your behaviors tell a lot about who you are and how you will perform in the classroom. Administrators want to know you outside of the highly crafted résumé and cover letter and your glowing references. In an interview, they get to know you by watching your mannerisms, your facial expressions, and your body language. They listen closely to your choice of words. They wonder how you will engage students, care for their learning, and deal with parents.

For this category, it is important to be as objective as possible. Take a look at yourself from outside of yourself. Schools are made up of students, faculty, employees, administration, parents, and the community at large. All of these people will be forming their opinions of you within the first few days or weeks of meeting you. You will develop a reputation quickly. And this reputation will last for years despite what you might say or do to alter it. Take a moment now to determine what it will be and make every relationship an opportunity to cultivate your reputation.

Being objective about how you behave and what your attitudes are is instructive. Without this self-evaluation, you might not see what the interviewing committee sees.

Determining Attitudes and Behaviors

There are many ways to self-evaluate. The following three tend to give a broad-enough spectrum.

Activity 1: The Imaginary Interview

Video record yourself being interviewed by a panel of educators as they ask you a series of questions. Watch the video and look at yourself objectively. Think about the person in the video as someone else. Watch the mannerisms, listen to the tone of voice, hear the words. What is that person communicating? What are his behaviors? What are her attitudes?

Consider them from the list below. Add any additional terms that do not appear on this list.

Activity 2: The Recorded Lesson

Video record (or audio record if video isn't appropriate) yourself teaching a lesson in a class. Watch the recording, and, again, observe yourself objectively as if that were some other teacher in the classroom. How would you evaluate that teacher's attitudes and behaviors? What does he say or do? How does she say or do it? Again, consider your attitudes and behaviors from the list below.

Activity 3: The School Social

Picture a seasonal event, like a fall festival where parents and children join faculty, employees, and administration for a social gathering at the school celebrating the start of the year. Who do you interact with? How do you interact? What do you say? What do you do? This activity sees you merging your professional self with your social self. Consider the behaviors and attitudes from the list below.

Table 2: Attitudes and behaviors

contemplative	fun	judgmental	popular
creative	generous	optimistic	rational
dynamic	honest	passionate	reflective
empathetic	humble	personable	serious
fair	innocent	playful	sophisticated

Bringing It All Together

In addition to the exercises above, your performance appraisals from your teacher practicums are instructive. Look to these for help in generating your complete list.

Collate these lists and rank the top few terms. Transfer these to the "My Personal Profile" at the end of this chapter.

Attitudes and Behaviors Reflection

What are your dominant attitudes and behaviors?

If you are an experienced educator or professional in a related field, then you have a very good sense of what attitudes and behaviors serve you well in your profession. If you are just transitioning to teaching, then you are at a pivotal moment, moving from student to teacher. Which of your attitudes and behaviors serve you best? Are there any you need to develop? Are there any you need to shed?

Work Habits

Your Work Habits

As a teacher, you will be evaluating student performance frequently in regard to work habits and learning skills. Recognizing how students work and how they learn is fundamental to guiding their growth and development.

In the same way, potential employers are evaluating each teacher candidate they interview and determining their work habits and learning skills. Whether they ask you directly in the interview or are inferring what your habits are based on what they see in your portfolio, you are being assessed according to the expectations employers have for their employees. *Is she the kind of person who will work independently and efficiently? Will he be the first one out the door at three thirty? Will she make a fuss when asked to change curriculum? Will he resist school policies?*

Knowing your dominant work habits and learning skills and anticipating what the employers are looking for in potential candidates sets you up for success.

Picture this: You research the school and discover that the administration places a high value on teams and working collaboratively. You genuinely believe yourself to possess these attributes and tailor your résumé and cover letter to include these terms. During the interview, you provide anecdotes about how you are a team player and work collaboratively and cooperatively with your colleagues. You develop rapport, built trust, and intrigue the employers. They are now closer to hiring you than ever before.

Chances are that at this stage in your life, you have had years of education, multiple job experiences, and a few volunteer activities, and you have probably participated as a leader or member of teams, clubs, bands, or various other activities. These are all great experiences from which to consider your dominant work habits.

Determining Work Habits

Consult the work habits table below. Which of the terms best describe you? Which best describe your approach to learning? Work habits in one area of our lives or in one job may differ significantly from those in another job. Take the time to consider these. Be honest with yourself. List only those that reflect who you are and the ones you most enjoy.

The three-pronged approach works best here.

The Personal Approach: Consult the work habits and learning skills table below. Check off any that describe you and add any that do not appear on the list. Prioritize these according to how effective you are at each.

The Friends and Family Approach: Your family and friends know you well. Ask them. Share the table to make their task easier.

The Professional Approach: Previous employers will probably have provided you with written feedback in the form of observations or performance appraisals. Consult these or ask current employers.

Table 3: Work habits and learning skills

accountable	diplomatic	listener	self-directed
adaptable	disciplined	organized	self-expressive
attentive	effective	prioritize	self-manager
collaborative	efficient	problem solver	self-regulator
contributor	empathetic	punctual	team player
cooperative	flexible	reliable	thinker
creative	independent	resourceful	thorough
decisive	initiative	responsible	time manager
determined	innovative	risk taker	versatile

Bringing It All Together

As with the values activity, you now have three lists: one that you generated personally, one that reflects your more social nature, and one that more closely reflects your professional persona. How do these compare? Are they closely aligned? Collate these lists and rank the top few. Transfer these to the "My Personal Profile" at the end of this chapter.

Work Habits and Learning Skills Reflection

What are your most dominant work habits and learning skills? How do these currently serve you? How do these help you become a better teacher? Where might you need to develop?

If you can accurately identify your dominant work habits and learning skills, then you can write much more articulate application documents. Résumés and cover letters are much more persuasive when they contain rich terminology.

In addition, interview questions target personality traits and interpersonal skills—among many other criteria. Having responses prepared that demonstrate you understand how you operate reveals to the panelists that you are conscientious and have a clarity of purpose.

Skills

The Importance of Your Skill Set

Have you ever considered all of the skills you have developed? Chances are your list is fairly extensive and you are capable of doing many diverse tasks.

High school introduced us to a variety of subjects and potential career opportunities. Undergraduate programs allowed us to narrow our focus and specialize in a particular field. Teachers' college programs narrowed the scope even further and guided us to target a particular discipline and age range. While each of these stages in our lives helped us become more and more skilled in one area, these also gave us a bit of tunnel vision. The more we focused our attention on one career goal, the more we refined our knowledge and talents and discarded a broader range of skills. This process of becoming more specialized in one area deceives us into believing we are not capable of achieving a wider range of skills.

Then this notion gets further compounded when we compare ourselves to others and shortchange ourselves on what we are capable of achieving. We often look to those people who are more successful or talented and discount our own abilities because we consider ourselves *not quite at that level.*

In considering our own talents, we have to take a much broader and more inclusive approach to all that we can do. Avoiding a limiting perspective helps us paint a much more vivid and realistic picture of who we are and what we are capable of.

Why Skills Matter

Why does it matter that you have had so many diverse experiences and developed such broad skills?

The education profession is looking for unique teachers who are accomplished in multiple disciplines, who can inspire and motivate students to pursue excellence, and who are willing to serve as role models.

Combing through all of your experiences and creating a comprehensive list of all your skills will help you in three ways. First of all, it will help you recognize all that you are capable of doing, giving you a sense of the breadth and depth of your life's experiences. Secondly, knowing what you have done will help you reflect and determine what you like doing. Finally, positioning yourself in such a way that you promote your best skills will reveal to potential employers that you are a talented person.

Determining Your Skills

Reflect on all of your experiences: education related, work related, and those of personal interest.

Education Skills

Begin with all of the skills you have acquired most recently in teacher's college and your undergraduate work and move in reverse order back through to high school.

Oftentimes, people discount the importance of the skills learned in high school because those were developed far too long ago in the past and do not really describe who they are now and what they are capable of achieving. But just because you have not done something for some time does not mean that that skill has atrophied. Given a little warm-up and a few practice sessions and you will, no doubt, be exhibiting that skill again. Cast a wide net and keep it all.

Work Experience Skills

This area comprises the second greatest area of skills. Chances are you have had multiple jobs over the years and developed significant skills in a broad range of areas.

A skill is a skill and often has transferability that is not always apparent. Don't discount any job you have had. Each is important. You might not want to promote it in your résumé or cover letter, but that doesn't eliminate the skill you have developed. Remember that you are putting together a comprehensive list all your skills.

Personal Interests

The third and final of these large areas of skill development is in your personal interests. Over the years, you will have tried many different hobbies, activities, sports, arts, music, and volunteer opportunities. Look to these as the third of the important areas for amassing a list of talents.

Teaching takes place not only in the classroom but in every interaction you have with students, whether on a sports field, a playground, or on the stage performing a play. Teachers are called upon to complete a multitude of activities. The richer your scope of experiences, the greater potential you have of securing that teaching position.

Table 4: Skills

analysis	information literacy	organization	social media
collaboration	interpersonal	planning	social
communication	interpreting	problem solving	teamwork
computer	leadership	productivity	technical
creativity	listening	public speaking	technology
critical thinking	management	reasoning	time management
design	media	research	verbal
efficiency	motivational	risk taking	writing

Bringing It All Together

Collate these lists and rank the top few terms. Transfer these to the "My Personal Profile" at the end of this chapter.

Skills Reflection

What are your dominant skills? Which serve you best in the teaching profession? Are there specific skills you have that you can leverage to your advantage? Are there skills you need to develop?

Differentiate, Differentiate, Differentiate

The purpose of this process is to leverage your profile in a way that captures the administrator's attention. If you showcase your range of values, work habits, attitudes, and talents, you have a greater likelihood of persuading administrators of your potential. Principals want to see talent in their schools. Show them what you are capable of achieving.

- Why did I go into teaching?
- What do I want to achieve in this profession?
- What's my outcome?
- Where do I see myself five years from now? Or ten years from now? Or twenty years from now?

My Personal Profile

My Values

1. _____
2. _____
3. _____
4. _____
5. _____
6. _____
7. _____
8. _____
9. _____
10. _____

My Attitudes and Behaviors

1. _____
2. _____
3. _____
4. _____
5. _____
6. _____
7. _____
8. _____
9. _____
10. _____

My Work Habits

1. _____
2. _____
3. _____
4. _____
5. _____
6. _____
7. _____
8. _____
9. _____
10. _____

My Competencies

1. _____
2. _____
3. _____
4. _____
5. _____
6. _____
7. _____
8. _____
9. _____
10. _____

Next Steps

The purpose of completing these tasks is to generate a comprehensive list of identifiers. If you have done the necessary self-analysis work and solicited support from family, friends, and other professionals, then you should have a very accurate personal profile. This process you have followed serves you in two fundamental ways in securing that teaching job.

First of all, this rich collection of terms is going to help tremendously in the process of writing your personal documents. Your cover letter and résumé are what get you an interview. Infusing these identifiers strategically throughout these documents will capture the attention of applicant-tracking software and administrators alike.

Secondly, in completing these self-analysis and scenario tasks, you have prepared for the interview. You will be asked these questions. Some will be explicitly targeted. Others will be implied.

In the next chapter, you will go about composing your teaching portfolio, transferring these values, habits, behaviors, and competencies to your professional documents. Well-written applications captivate the readers and persuade them to take a step further and offer you an interview.

Let's take this next step.

————————————————————————————

CHAPTER 5

Your Professional Portfolio

Purpose

Teacher portfolios are an extension of the job application. If you have secured an interview, then your portfolio showcases who you are as an educator, giving the panelists more information to help them make a decision. Well-composed portfolios are rich reflections of your complete character.

Contents

The contents of a teacher portfolio are determined by the job prospect. Comprehensive and complete portfolios tailored for the school or school district get the most attention. These portfolios suggest the applicant has taken care to study the job description and the school climate and customized the portfolio with the recipients in mind.

Comprehensive and complete portfolios contain two separate sets of work. Professional documents comprise the first half of the portfolio, and examples of work comprise the second. Examples of work are very specific to you and what you have done in the classroom. Professional documents are broad and applicable to everyone. The scope of this book is in developing professional documents.

Samples of lesson and unit plans, tasks, assessments and evaluations, and teacher observations are all part of a professional portfolio. These follow your professional documents. However, these are very specific to your individual practices in the subjects and grades you teach and are outside the range of the documents required.

Professional Documents
1. Professional goals
2. Personal statement
3. Teaching philosophy
4. Cover letter
5. Résumé
6. Professional brand
7. Reference letters

Samples of Work
1. Lesson plans
2. Unit plans
3. Multiple assessments (e.g., activities, tests)
4. Rich performance tasks
5. Student observations (e.g., anecdotal comments)
6. Student evaluations (e.g., report card comments)
7. Teacher observations (e.g., performance appraisals)
8. Photographs (e.g., classroom layout)

Step 1: Your Professional Goals

Purpose
Taking the time to reflect on your personal interests and setting goals in an effort to continually learn and improve is an excellent way to reveal to prospective employers that you are focused and deliberate in your actions. A breadth of interests and goals also reveals a multitalented individual, and this impresses employers.

Essential Questions
- What do you intend to accomplish in your teaching career?
- How do you want to develop as an educator?
- How will you continue to stay current?
- What obstacles do you foresee and how will you handle them?

- Where do you see yourself five or ten years from now?

Introduction

Education is as much about teaching as it is about learning. As an educator, you consider the curriculum that needs to be covered; you think about the needs of the students; you wonder which methods of delivery will allow you to best address the expectations and the needs of the students; you develop tasks and assessments that will satisfy these demands; you deliver them; you reflect on their effectiveness and success; you redeliver or fill in the gaps as needed; and then you evaluate student learning. While there are many idiosyncratic elements to this process, it is, for the most part, complete. Some of this process is teaching. But much of it really is learning. You are continually learning through planning and implementing—trial and error—what is most effective and what isn't.

This is one of the most appealing aspects of education. Despite the amount of experience in the classroom, there will always be opportunities for learning and growing as a teacher. Teaching is dynamic, just as learning is dynamic. There is a constancy of flux in the whole process. Content may or may not remain the same. Methods of delivering content change. Tasks can have greater appeal, reach more curriculum expectations, and engage more students. And evaluation methods continually get more refined.

School administrators have very limited information on prospective candidates. They might have résumés and cover letters, but these are only snapshots of the real person. There is a finite amount of information that can be shared in the present job-application process. A goal page in your portfolio solves this problem. Having a clear set of goals lets the reader know the value you place on continual growth and improvement.

Who would you hire following an interview? Someone who shared his professional goals and was clear about what areas he needed to focus on? Or someone who could not really answer the question, "What goals do you have for your first year of teaching with us?" What will you respond when asked the common question, "What do you see yourself doing five years from now?"

Goal Setting

Goal setting can take the form of a single initiative or multiple initiatives simultaneously. Some goals are improvement oriented, as in tweaking or fine-tuning something already known. Others are breakthrough goals in which a whole new skill is tackled. As well, goals can be short-term, intermediate-term, or long-term.

Teachers are in a unique position to goal set. Experienced teachers can always refine their practices or take on new initiatives like a different grade, subject, or school. Summer breaks offer opportunities to reflect on the past year, recharge, and consider the future. Every September brings with it a new school year, and every new school year offers the potential for growth and change.

New teachers have many skills to develop and are at a critical stage as they transition from being students to becoming professionals. There is a lot to learn and practice. Invariably, new teachers tackle a host of new initiatives in a variety of areas in this on-the-job training process.

Whether as a new or experienced teacher, change and adapting to change is inevitable in the teaching profession, especially with the impact of technology, social media, and the democratization of learning. Teachers need to be ready to leave their comfort zones, learn new material, and apply new skills. Annual goal setting makes getting out of comfort zones comfortable.

Setting goals and achieving goals also serves as great modeling for students. We ask students to set goals on a yearly basis—if not more frequently. Certainly, we model appropriate habits, attitudes, and values, but when we model goal setting and achievement, we demonstrate that learning is lifelong, that at any age or stage in life, a person can take on a new challenge, learn a new skill, or adopt a new perspective.

Areas for Goal Setting

Goal setting for the teacher professional can manifest in any number of ways. After all, as teachers, we want to get better at what we do so that we can improve our efficiency, master our subject matter, or increase our rapport with students. A more deliberate approach to goal setting is to categorize goals under specific headings. Having three general categories allows us to focus on multiple initiatives and keeps us thinking and acting on them.

While there are a variety of headings that can be used, this three-pronged approach works effectively: professional goals, career goals, and personal goals.

Professional goals relate to your competence and expertise as an educator and are typically about improving teaching practice and directly affecting the students in the classroom. For instance, learning how to develop a rubric that meets specific criteria will help you narrow what you are looking for in the task as well as clarify to students what the objectives and outcomes of the task are. Professional goals serve as great anecdotes during interviews or in your portfolio package because they reveal how you are a reflective practitioner and that improving your practice is important to you.

Career goals are not about directly benefiting the students but are about benefiting you. Will you upgrade your qualifications? Take on a master's or PhD program? Learn to teach theatre? These are goals aimed primarily at benefiting you. Yes, in the long run, they will ultimately benefit students, but at the outset, you are thinking about your own career. Taking on each of the above, for instance, is something you can add to your résumé. Career goals serve you first.

Personal goals differ from professional and career goals. These are the kinds of goals you want to pursue because they are of interest to you. They may be about athletics, arts, travel, service, or a multitude of other topics. They are intended to serve you only. Will you take up sushi prep, SLR photography, or skydiving?

Of course, there is also a difference between public and private goals; the former, you are willing to share with a potential employer, while the latter you are not. Which will you share?

What Is the Right Number of Goals to Pursue?
There are different schools of thought on how many goals to pursue at once. If you are tackling a breakthrough goal that encompasses hours of your day, then that might be just enough. But if you find that you have many small initiatives, it may be easier to work on multiple goals

simultaneously. Ultimately, you have to answer the question: *what am I comfortable with?*

Timeline for Goal Achievement

Short-Term Goals

Short-term goals for the teacher professional are best set with a one- to three-year time horizon. In your first year of teaching, you are learning how to teach—specifically in that grade, those subjects, and that school. In the second year, you are tweaking what you attempted in the first, improving upon some elements, adding others, and discarding those that didn't work as well. And in the third year, you are beginning to master these, having gone through the process twice already. With each year, you become increasingly more proficient with the planning process, the subject matter, and the evaluation methods, as well as with establishing a healthy learning environment, building rapport with students, and working collegially.

Short-term goals typically focus on learning how to teach a particular subject or grade. Sometimes teachers need to relearn the subject matter themselves before they can teach it. Then they need to learn how to teach it effectively. Many experienced teachers will say that teaching a particular subject isn't the difficult part. What is most difficult is understanding what students need at that age and how best to meet those needs. Short-term goals, then, can be about identifying areas of growth for you if you are a novice teacher.

Sample short-term goals include the following:

- securing a position as a grade-four homeroom teacher in a prestigious elementary school
- developing and improving classroom systems to keep organized
- improving discipline strategies focusing on discipline with dignity
- increasing parental contact through monthly phone calls and regular e-mails

Areas to consider in short-term goal planning include the following:

- curriculum planning
- assessing and evaluating
- reporting
- the learning environment
- classroom management
- classroom organization
- coaching and supervising
- interacting with students
- interacting with parents
- working with colleagues

Intermediate-Term Goals

Intermediate-term goals are those set with a longer time horizon and typically run from the three to seven years. These goals encompass a broad range of areas and include professional development. Moving to a new grade level, a new subject, or a new school are all worthy ventures. Each time a new grade or subject or school is begun, the process of mastery starts over again: you begin as a new teacher, you develop, you become proficient, and you master. Attending workshops and conferences and taking additional qualification courses are all instructive and helpful in leading you through this growth process.

But so too are running your own workshops and conferences. If you have just learned and practiced a new skill, you are in a prime position to teach others. Putting your thoughts together in a coherent manner can help you solidify your understanding of the strategy or technique. Teachers are always wanting to learn *best practices* from their colleagues because it saves them the time and effort of trying something new with the fear that it might fail. If you have gone through the learning process, then you can serve the teaching community well by sharing your learning.

Intermediate-term goals are also in that transition zone between professional goals and career goals. You might find you want to continually focus on your professional goal and continually tweak what you do well or make switches in grades or subjects within the same division or school. Or you might look at bigger career changes. Moving out of the classroom is a career goal. Attaining the level of principal, trustee, or professor is beyond the professional goal realm.

Sample intermediate-term goals include the following:

- switching to the intermediate division and teaching grade-eight science and math
- taking the three-part specialist courses over a series of summers
- achieving principal papers
- pursuing a master's or PhD
- training as an assistant varsity basketball coach

Areas to consider in intermediate-term goal planning include the following:

- grade switch
- school switch
- subject switch
- assistant role
- workshop/conference leader
- management position
- mentoring new teachers
- junior leadership position

Long-Term Goals

Long-term goals are any that last longer than approximately seven years. The long-term horizon approaches much quicker than it might initially appear. It is easy to get wrapped up in improving your teaching practice year after year until suddenly it seems that a decade has passed. There is a common expression among teachers that *the day is long, but the year is short.*

Knowing what you want to do ten years from now seems as though it might be too far in the future to even consider. But as the years race by, you will want to have a clear picture of what you will be doing in the future. Would you like to move into administration and leave the classroom partially? Would you like to move out of the classroom entirely and lead schools or school districts?

These are *big-idea* questions and hardly answerable by someone whose primary objective is to get her first teaching job. However, having at least a vague idea of what you would like to accomplish in your teaching career goes far with administrators who want to know how well you have considered the teaching profession and what you would like to accomplish in your life.

There's nothing wrong with your long-term goal being to remain in the same grade, in the same school, teaching the same subject if this is what you want to do. Knowing that this is your goal is what is important. Clarity is key.

Sample long-term goals include the following:

- becoming a principal
- leading a school
- becoming a resource specialist
- gaining membership on the board of your local college of teachers

Areas to consider in your long-term goal planning include the following:

- leadership position in a school: principal / vice principal
- trustee on local board
- teacher's college instructor
- private school leadership

From Goals to Actions

Goal setting can be very enjoyable. There is this sense that anything is possible when you dream about what you would like to achieve. Turning dreams into reality requires a plan and a commitment to see the goals through to their completion. The following are common strategies that goal achievers share. Implementing a few of these will produce dramatic results.

Top Ten Strategies for Goal Achievement

1. **Write Out Your Goals.** People who articulate their goals in written form are more likely to achieve them. Writing goals forces you to think through them, and the more you think through the goals, the better the plans you develop for their attainment.

2. **Use the SMART Mnemonic.** Make your goals *specific, measurable, attainable, realistic,* and *time based.*

3. **Set Incremental Steps.** Draw a road map outlining the steps that need to be taken in order to achieve your goals. Accomplish each step along the way until the goals are achieved.

4. **Keep the Goals Visible.** Keep the goals on your screen to be reminded of them whenever you turn on your computer. Have them on your phone. Post them weekly in your calendar so they pop up regularly. Write them on a sheet of paper and keep them in your pocket, wallet, or purse.

5. **Write Your Goals Out Daily.** Keep a journal handy and write out your goals on a daily basis. You will find you have them foremost on your mind, and the more you think about them, the more you move yourself to do something about them.

6. **Use a Multisensory Approach.** Write out your goals, read them aloud, and recite them aloud. Keep your mind thinking, writing, reading, and saying your goals, and you will continually come closer to achieving them.

7. **Have an Accountability Friend.** Hold yourself responsible for achieving your goals by sharing them with a friend or two. Have them check on you repeatedly to ensure you are working toward achieving each goal.

8. **Hire a Coach.** Get a professional coach who can encourage and push you along. Coaches who are in the particular field can guide you through the process, anticipate pitfalls, check accuracy, correct progress, focus you, and motivate you.

9. **Track Your Accomplishments.** Every successful goal achieved is a victory. Every time a contact is made, a concept learned, or a skill developed is a testament to your efforts. Build momentum by tracking your accomplishments.

10. **Celebrate Your Achievements.** Rewards are effective reminders of why we do things. Celebrate small and large victories.

Step 2: Your Unique Personal Statement

Purpose

The personal statement is a declaration of who you are and what you intend to do in your professional career. It is a clear and confident testament of your deepest interests, skills, and values.

Personal statements are often used when applying to college and university programs. These are screening documents that schools use to vet out potential students in their programs. Graduate programs require a commitment of time and money from you, and they want to be certain you are making the *right* decision for the *right* reasons.

This is a worthy exercise for the teacher candidate who needs to reason through her decision to pursue teaching and to pursue a particular job at a school or school district. Personal statements force us to think through our decision making and reason why we are choosing to teach a specific grade and subject. The more you can work through this before applying for a teaching position, the more likely it is that you apply for a position that is the best fit for you.

A personal statement is often written as a response to a multilayered question with specific parameters for content and length. Writing your own and directing it to the school or school district for which you are applying helps to clarify your intents and focus your efforts. This activity further helps you articulate responses and solidify answers to questions you will be asked during the interview.

Because it does not require the enormous detail of a résumé, nor the formality of the cover letter, the personal statement allows for much more individual expression.

Instructions for Writing a Personal Statement

Here are three simple prompts to follow:

- Write a one-page essay in which you defend who you are, what you intend to do with your life, and why teaching is the right profession for you. Your essay should contain a well-articulated and focused goal followed by a presentation of your skill set, your character traits, your values, and your competencies.
- In a one-page essay, explain why you want to teach at this specific school. Consider your educational experience, your work experience, and your personal interests. Answer the question, *why should this school hire you?*
- In three hundred words, explain why you want to teach. Consider your values, your experiences, and your skills. How will these contribute to your success and make you an effective teacher?

Three Approaches to Writing Your Personal Statement

While there is a lot of freedom in writing a personal statement, maintaining a specific approach to its composition helps ground and direct your writing. Consider one of the following three directions:

- **The Professional Educator Approach.** With this approach in mind, you want to focus on your values, skill set, and behavior and how these all reveal you to be a professional educator. Scope the standards of practice from your associated college of teachers for terms and concepts. There is rich terminology to help you express yourself as a professional educator.

- **The Student-Centered Approach.** As teaching is essentially about students, focusing your personal statement on how students are at the center of your teaching practice captures the attention of prospective employers—especially when applying to preschool, primary, and junior divisions where students are less independent and require more attention and direction from their teachers.

- **The School Community Approach.** This third approach focuses on the community as a complete entity with all its constituents: students, faculty, administration, employees, parents, families, and local organizations. Each member plays an important role, and yours is significant in the context of this education community. If your interest is to work in a boarding school, this would be an important approach to consider.

Write your personal statement with your audience in mind. Be prepared to include this in your portfolio and share it with any prospective employers. Personal statements are viewed by administrators like résumés and cover letters. They may only spend thirty seconds reading them, but those thirty seconds count. If you can compel the reader to take a closer look, then you stand a greater chance of holding her captive. Every little bit counts when you are aiming for your ideal teaching job.

Top Ten Tips for Writing a Unique Personal Statement

1. **Honest Portrayal.** The best personal statements are those that reveal character and integrity. Be honest; be forthright. Reveal your interests and your beliefs.

2. **Professional.** Everything you write, how you write it, where you post it, with whom you share it should all be *as if* it were to be viewed by an interview panel. Raise the level of professionalism in your writing and you increase your chances of success.

3. **Goal Specific.** Clearly articulate your most important professional goals. Choose carefully from your short-, intermediate-, and long-term goals.

4. **Presents a Road Map.** A goal is only as good as the strategy used to achieve it. Provide the direction you intend to take. Clear steps to achievement reveal careful thought and consideration. To the administrator, this shows focus and resolve—admirable qualities in a teacher candidate.

5. **Reveals Values.** Share your values to make a more personal connection with the reader.

6. **Highlights Achievements.** Share a few diverse achievements. Consider any risk-taking tasks or challenges overcome. Teachers modeling this behavior act as strong role models of learning as a lifelong process.

7. **Complete.** Every document has its purpose. A personal statement should be complete and leave no room for ambiguity or uncertainty.

8. **Compelling and Endearing.** Draw out the best in you, and be appealing to the reader.

9. **Visually Appealing.** Make the work visually accessible and easily readable. Keep the personal statement to one page, and balance the layout. Too much information in a poorly laid out work is unpleasant and turns the reader off. The rule *less is more* applies here.

10. **Enduring Character.** You have the potential in your personal values, goals, and achievements to relate a very enduring character—one that administrators will remember long after having read your portfolio. Captivate the reader and make yourself memorable.

Step 3: Your Distinct Teaching Philosophy

Purpose

Every educator has a teaching philosophy. Each of us has opinions and beliefs about many different aspects of our profession. However, we don't always record our thoughts. This becomes a challenge when we are questioned in an interview about a particular aspect we have not articulated in words. From the employer's point of view, this hesitation is just enough to cause a sense of uncertainty in our capacity to be successful educators.

Teaching philosophies solve the problem and improve your opportunities because they force you to consider every aspect of the profession and to articulate your thoughts in words. The more decisive you are in your interview responses, the more influential you become with the interview panel. The more you can prepare effectively for the interview by developing a comprehensive teaching philosophy before that moment in the hot seat, the more you will present with conviction. Certainty in the applicant increases confidence in the interviewer.

As with the personal statement, a teaching philosophy adds credibility to your character. Securing your dream job requires you to present yourself as *outstanding*. Outstanding portfolios contain outstanding contents, including a unique personal statement and a distinct teaching philosophy.

Teacher's college programs often ask incoming faculty to consider their teaching philosophy. The responses submitted tend to be highly idealistic based on personal musings and reflections of the student's own experiences with education. However, if you are a recent teacher's college graduate, then you have been exposed to an array of aspects in this profession and have formed many opinions about each. New faculty tend to be ardent, showing great promise and admiration for the profession. On the other hand, if you have been teaching for some time, then you are fortunate in having solidified much of your philosophy already. Practiced faculty tend to use their experiences to guide their philosophy—their notions honed through trial.

Whether it is a highly idealistic philosophy or one honed from experience, it should be comprehensive in scope.

Instructions for Developing Your Teaching Philosophy

Consider each category below. Let the questions guide your thinking about the topic. Record your responses. Can you prioritize each concept according to its relevance or importance to you?

Students

- Who is the ideal student?
- How do you feel about high achievers who require constant challenge?
- How do you feel about students who struggle and require constant remediation?
- What are your thoughts on English language learners?
- What role do special education students play in the general classroom?

Learning Environment

- What do you value in a classroom layout?
- How does your classroom layout engender an ideal learning environment?
- How do you motivate students?

Classroom Management

- What rules do you have for your classroom?
- How do you value processes and procedures?
- How is authority in the classroom manifested?
- What kind of leadership is present in the classroom?
- How does an effective classroom present?
- How is behavior managed?

Discipline

- What role does discipline play in the classroom?
- How are behavioral issues handled?
- Which discipline methods are most effective? Why?
- How do you ensure that discipline leaves a student's dignity intact?

Teaching and Learning
- What teaching strategies appeal most to you?
- What teaching strategies do you find most effective?
- How do you learn about and employ best practices?

Curriculum Knowledge and Planning
- What planning process do you follow?
- How do you ensure you plan with learning outcomes in mind?
- How do you leverage school resources?
- How do you ensure you are planning effectively?

Assessment and Evaluation
- What is the purpose of assessment?
- What is the purpose of evaluation?
- What assessments best meet curriculum expectations or learning outcomes?
- How do you ensure assessments are varied in form?
- How do you ensure assessments are rich performance tasks capturing knowledge and skills?
- Are your assessments results-oriented?
- Are your assessments innovative?

People Skills
- How do you work with colleagues?
- What role do your colleagues play in your own teachings?
- What is your relationship with your supervisors (vice principals or principals)?
- What do you believe the role of vice principals and principals to be in your classroom?

Role of Parents
- What do you believe the role of parents to be in their child's education?

- Where does your role as teacher and their role as parents overlap?
- How can you leverage parental interest effectively to improve your teaching?

Communication Skills
- Where do you find your communication strengths highest? In speaking? In writing?
- Are you an effective listener? Or effective speaker?
- How frequently do you communicate home?
- Do you call? E-mail? Create newsletters? Post messages?

School Community
- What role does the greater school community play in your classroom?
- How do you leverage the school community to engage students and teach effectively?

Communication Technology and Social Media
- What role does communication technology play in your subject and your classroom?
- What role does social media play in your classroom?

Contents of the Teaching Philosophy

What happened as you recorded your thoughts on each topic? Did you find some easier to write about than others? Have you had more experience with some? Where do you identify your greatest competence?

Writing a teaching philosophy requires reflecting on each topic, organizing thoughts, and communicating them clearly and persuasively. There is so much to talk about and far too much to capture in a succinct one-page statement. While there is no rule about what to include, general practice suggests discussing people, places, and processes. Consider selecting from the following and including them in your statement:

- a general teaching and learning statement
- a specific student statement

- strategies you employ for building student rapport
- how you would set up the optimal learning environment
- your planning practices and methods
- your specific teaching practices
- what you believe the role of assessment and evaluation to be
- effective strategies you have used for classroom management
- the role of discipline in the classroom
- effective parent relations and strategies for including parents in the learning process
- strategies for leveraging communications technology and social media to improve learning
- techniques for building a team mentality as well as leadership capacity in students
- recognizing the role of administrators in your classroom
- strategies for leveraging the school community to improve your teaching

Approaches to Writing a Teaching Philosophy
The People Approach
Teaching philosophies that center heavily on people are dominated by thoughts about students, parents, colleagues, and administration. In this approach, people are at the center of education.

The Places Approach
Teaching philosophies that address the place are dominated by thoughts of the learning environment, the school as a physical building, the school district, and the location. They focus on the environment as most conducive to teaching and student success.

The Processes Approach
Teaching philosophies that heavily address processes are dominated by thoughts about the process of teaching and include resources, planning, instruction, and assessment and evaluation. These focus on developing an optimal process for learning.

No one approach is foolproof. Handled strategically, all three can be incorporated.

Top Ten Tips for Writing a Distinct Teaching Philosophy

1. **Deliberately Ordered.** Prioritize your top few points about teaching. For instance, if you decided to become a teacher because you enjoy the collegial nature of the profession or you like putting psychological theory into practice, state it. Be decisive.

2. **Comprehensive in Scope.** Let the administration know how thorough you are by covering all significant aspects of the profession.

3. **Demonstrates Competence.** Prove your knowledge and understanding of each aspect of teaching through your use of key teaching terminology.

4. **Reveals Passion for Teaching.** What you say and how you say it should reveal a love of teaching.

5. **Makes Students the Central Focus of Education.** This should appear abundantly clear: a primary focus for educators is to help children succeed in life. State it.

6. **Goes beyond the Curriculum.** There are many opportunities to build a child's character. Often, these moments happen outside of the class and outside subject curricula. Address how your role as a teacher goes beyond the classroom.

7. **Addresses the Roles of All Stakeholders.** There are many people involved in raising children, including teachers, administrators, specialists, and, of course, parents. Reveal your knowledge of the scope of an educator's role by incorporating these other people as assisting you in achieving your goals.

8. **Demonstrates a Desire to Learn.** Teachers learn what works through trial and error. Demonstrating that you are a reflective practitioner shows your desire to continually improve your performance.

9. **Make It Distinct.** Everyone has his or her own personal opinions and beliefs about teaching. Distinguish yourself from others. Display your original thoughts.

10. **Reveals Professionalism.** Everything about your teaching philosophy should communicate professionalism: your content, your word choice, your writing style.

Step 4: Your Exceptional Résumé

Purpose

The purpose of a résumé is to provide a detailed summary of all of your life's experiences in a structured and formulaic manner. It is a snapshot of you to date and includes your most admirable character traits, your applicable teaching skills, your educational experience, and your work history, among other elements. At its core, it is one profile of you complete with distinct and discrete categories. Résumés serve the purpose of giving the most accurate overview of all you have accomplished professionally within a two-page limit. They can appear rich in terminology and broad in experience but also dry and impersonal. Résumés are the mathematics and sciences of applications, and cover letters the literature.

Your résumé is the most important application document for hiring committees. It should be prepared deliberately, patiently, and strategically. Nothing should appear on the résumé that's not directed to the job for which you are applying. Any extraneous information is a hindrance.

Treating the résumé with the care it demands is equal to preparing effectively for the teacher interview. Too little attention to its formality and structure suggests carelessness and a lack of desire for the job.

There are many approaches to the composition of an effective résumé with many examples online. Using these to guide your own writing is an excellent approach, but take care to ensure that the model clearly allows you to capture who you are. Restrictive formats could be limiting.

The personal profile you developed in chapter 4 is instrumental to your writing of both your résumé and cover letter. Devoting a section of your résumé to communicating your core values and core competencies identifies to the reader your most significant character traits. Employers want to know you. If you tell them up front, then it makes the process of interviewing you easier. As you respond to questions, you validate these character traits. To employers, this is assurance that what you say about yourself in the interview is consistent with what you wrote about yourself in the résumé. Once again, clarity and confidence is conviction.

Top Ten Tips for Writing an Exceptional Résumé

1. **Broad in Scope.** Great résumés manage to capture a wide range of material, including contact information, professional goals, relevant character traits, education, career highlights, work experience, volunteer practice, and personal interests. Sometimes even more is added, including awards, committees, and pertinent organizations.

2. **Thorough in Detail.** Administrators want to know what you are like in the work environment. They want to know that you possess the character traits but also that you have had the practice or experience that would lead to a successful transition and functioning in the position. Provide detail about your practicum and any teaching-related experiences.

3. **Selective and Focused.** An exceptional résumé for the teaching professional is specific and targeted to the school or school district. You will have had a variety of experiences and possibly a host of different jobs over the years. Only those that are relevant to the teaching profession should be included, and the more you can align these with the school to which you are applying, the better.

4. **Organized and Ordered.** Strategically organized résumés in an order that highlights important aspects of the teacher professional are necessary for the document to get the desired attention. You might spend hours or weeks composing your résumé, but administrators will spend seconds reading it. Make what you write count.

5. **Formal in Writing Style.** Résumés need to communicate professionalism. There is no room for clichés, colloquialisms, and casual or informal language. Sophisticate your style.

6. **Use of the Active Voice.** Every bullet point must begin with an action verb. Bullet points are about your actions—what you do for current jobs and what you did for past jobs. Administrators want to know that you are a person of action.

7. **Free of Errors.** Résumés must be well written. No errors in grammar, spelling, or punctuation. This is a must. Spell check, grammar check, and proofread repeatedly.

8. **Visually Appealing Layout.** Style, font, and size all need careful attention. Too much and overly done can appear gaudy while too little reveals a lack of effort or knowledge of effective presentation strategies.

9. **Effective Use of Page Real Estate.** Too much text and no one will want to read your résumé, while too little suggests a weak and inexperienced candidate not worthy of further pursuit. The optimal résumé balances text with blank space.

10. **Electronically Capable.** Despite how visually appealing and well presented your résumé may appear, make sure it can function effectively as an electronic document. If filtering programs cannot search your résumé, your chances of exposure are significantly reduced.

Step 5: Your Outstanding Cover Letter

Purpose

Your cover letter represents you and the kind of professional teacher you will become. A poorly composed and articulated cover letter suggests a haphazard and careless regard for the form and will likely be viewed by the hiring committee with the same amount of effort put into writing it. An exceptionally well-written letter draws the attention of the reader, captivates her, and sustains her interest through to the end. This is the kind of cover letter you want representing you.

As with the résumé, the cover letter answers the question: *why should I hire you?*

Visualize yourself as a member of a hiring committee reading dozens of cover letters and looking for gems. The three of you sit around a table discussing all of the pros and cons of each applicant. You hear from your colleagues that they don't like the way some of the candidates have used casual or conversational language or how they were a little too informal in their writing style, taking many liberties in the word choice, tone, or sentence structure. They dismiss all of these candidates because if these people cannot take the time to put together a formal cover letter, then what will they do on a daily basis in the classroom? What will their lesson plans be like? How will they treat the students?

Teaching is a profession, and presenting yourself as a professional in all your communication is essential.

Top Ten Tips for Writing an Outstanding Cover Letter

1. **Engaging and Persuasive.** Your cover letter should capture the administrator's attention and sustain it. The ultimate goal is to persuade him to meet with you for an interview.

2. **Compelling.** *Who are you? Why are you worth my time? How can you serve our community?* Present a compelling picture of yourself that makes an administrator want to learn more about you and meet you in person.

3. **Sincere and Authentic.** Be careful of boasting and overinflating your accomplishments. Truth and honesty reveal integrity.

4. **Teacher Terminology.** A convincing cover letter demonstrates an understanding of the key terms educators use as well as the current issues they face.

5. **Formal in Writing Style.** As stated above, résumés need to communicate professionalism, and so too do cover letters. There is no room for clichés, colloquialisms, casual or informal language. Sophisticate your style here also.

6. **Anticipates the Administrator's Concerns.** Administrators have a host of thoughts, including, *How will this person handle difficult students in the classroom? Can she manage a full class with multiple learning abilities? How will her colleagues perceive her? Is she worth our time?* Dispelling concerns of the administrator is one purpose of the cover letter. This letter should anticipate the fear and concerns of the hiring committee and present a person of confidence and competence.

7. **Presents Supporting Details.** Statements without details or proof appear as an inflation of ego without substance. Your cover letter should provide sufficient detail to confirm your statements. Examples of experiences you have had solidify your character.

8. **Share an Anecdote.** Stories are memorable. Take the time to craft a very brief story that highlights a particular trait that will leave the committee thinking of you.

9. **Reveals a Genuine Interest in Students.** If your cover letter does not reveal that you have a genuine interest in helping students learn and grow, then the committee is left wondering why you entered this profession if not for the children. An effective cover letter embraces the notion that children are at the center of your desire to teach.

10. **Use Emotional Appeal.** The purpose of the cover letter is to *move* the reader to take action and interview you. Administrators want competence in their faculty, but they also want passionate educators. Reveal your passion.

Step 6: Your Professional Brand Image

Purpose

Social media is becoming an increasingly necessary component of the application process given our significant online presence. Leveraged effectively, it can land you an interview and a job.

At this point in the application process, you have completed all of the necessary documents you will use to apply for a teaching position as well as include in your professional portfolio. It is now time to brand yourself professionally through social media.

Completing this step is important to your success, as you run the risk of jeopardizing your opportunities if you don't take care to recognize what employers already see when they search your name on the web. Rarely does an employer not do this. It just makes sense to do so. Employers don't want to waste countless hours pursuing candidates who will not work out in the long run. They want to know everything up front. You might reveal a completely professional personality in your application documents, but you might also reveal character traits in your social media that cause employers to hesitate on pursuing you further.

If you are somewhat intimidated by the thought of branding yourself and self-promotion, then consider this an exercise in putting your portfolio online. Promoting yourself via social media is an important step to achieving your dream job. See this as an opportunity to present yourself professionally in an increasingly preferred medium.

Your Professional Brand

Building a professional brand shouldn't seem onerous. Your brand is what you have already completed in your personal statement and teaching philosophy. These are your values, your attitudes and behaviors, your work habits, and your competencies. Each of these defines you. These are your professional brand.

Process Overview: Scrutinize, Purge, and Begin Anew
Building your brand image online requires three simple steps: first of all, examining what is already posted; secondly, deciding what stays and purging the rest; and thirdly, building your professional persona.

Contents of Your Social Media Sites
There are three main elements that identify you online: images, videos, and text. Scrutinizing each of these three on all platforms will help you align your social presence with the professional image you want to convey.

Look at your social media from the perspective of a parent whose child will be entering your grade-three class next year. Go to each social media page you have and look at each photo, each video, and each bit of text you have posted. Could you imagine what the response would be if this parent saw these? Would the parent question your ability as an educator? Do these inspire confidence in you? Would the parent see you as friendly, caring, and nurturing? Consider also what a potential employer would do if she came across these. Would the parent question your level of professionalism or write you off as young, immature, and not ready for the world of teaching?

Look for your name on multiple search engines to be thorough. You may need to contact friends and ask them to take down material if they have tagged your name on photos that don't fit your professional image.

Your LinkedIn Account
There are a host of great social media sites that, used effectively, can position you for success. If you don't already have a LinkedIn account, get one. It is a must. There is really no question. If there is only one social media site you are willing to share publicly, then make it LinkedIn. Not only does it serve as an extension of your résumé and cover letter, but it also has many features that further enhance your profile, which traditional documents cannot offer.

This is where you want to be online.

As it continues to evolve, it is proving to be an invaluable resource for employers who may become increasingly dependent on its multiple features. Consider LinkedIn the central hub where you will develop your professional brand. All other sites will mirror aspects of what you communicate here. With its many features, you can leverage LinkedIn in ways that will increase your visibility and showcase your talent.

The Features

There are many aspects to your LinkedIn profile that can serve as extensions of the portfolio you have already produced. Transferring this material to your LinkedIn profile is all that is required.

However, there are a few areas that need further consideration: your photo, your summary, your experiences, your skills and endorsements, and your connections.

1. **Photo.** Choose a photo that reveals your professionalism— consider wearing conservative clothing and putting on a welcoming smile. Avoid casual clothing, copious makeup, and hair or facial accessories. Your photo is a first impression for employers. Treat this the way you would dress for an interview.

2. **Summary.** The summary is an opportunity for you to tell your story in 150–300 words. This story could be in first person or third person but should be a succinct overview of who you are and what you have been doing until this moment. Keep the statements broad and general. Let them provide interest and compel the viewer to read on.

   I like to think of this section as the first formal question of an interview in which the committee says, "Tell us a little about yourself." If you are a recent graduate, then your response could be about your professional experience, what you have been doing by way of your undergraduate degree, your postgraduate studies, your teacher's college experience, and your practicums. You could highlight many of the opportunities that you have had working with children or students in day care facilities, camps, and schools. If you are transitioning into the teaching profession or are an experienced teacher, then consider sharing highlights from your various accomplishments in these other areas or schools.

3. **Experience.** The experience section, essentially, is your résumé. Here you will simply upload all that you have in your résumé, including *experience*, *honors and awards*, *skills*, *language*, and *education*. There's nothing challenging to this section. You have already drafted your résumé and tweaked your language. Simply *cut and paste*.

4. **Skills and Endorsements.** Endorsements are the reference realm of the LinkedIn world. While these will not serve to the degree of formal references, consider these valuable opportunities for someone else to speak highly of you and tout your talents.

5. **Connections.** Once you have a completed LinkedIn profile, begin making connections with many people from a host of different professions in order to build up your sphere and increase your network. This is a great advantage of LinkedIn. You can become connected with many people from many disciplines, and the more connections you make, the broader your reach. Opportunities are everywhere. Cast a wide net in your connections.

Who You Should Connect With

Colleagues. Your colleagues should be among the first of the connections you make. If you have just completed teacher's college, then connect with all your college colleagues. After all, you worked together through teacher's college. Maintaining these relationships through the job search process will prove beneficial.

Supervising Teachers. Connect with any educators you worked closely with in your teacher practicums. If there were supervisory teachers who you reported to or teachers who evaluated you during this period of time, you should request a connection with them. They may serve you well, as they will have many professional connections.

Educational Professionals. What about professors, instructors, or teaching assistants? If you have a good working relationship with these people and would be willing to ask them for a written recommendation, then you should ask them to connect with you.

The Power of Connections. Having connections means you have contact with people who might be influential with employers. They themselves may be responsible for hiring or they may be able to connect you with employers. There is no harm in asking.

6. **Other Features.** Consider broadening your reach through LinkedIn's *Groups, Following, Projects, Organizations,* and *Volunteering and Causes* features.

Step 7: Your Letters of Reference

Purpose

The purpose of a reference letter is for a credible person to support you in your job-application process. Reference letters attest to your personal character and your competence as an educator. Essentially, they say to the committee that you are worth hiring.

But you don't write your own reference letters and have little control over what is written about you.

Nevertheless, there is much that you can do to manage the content of the reference letter. Providing the reference with quality material that can be used in the letter is not only essential but also welcomed by the writer. Share your portfolio with your reference. Talk to him about your goals. Or let her briefly interview you, asking a few questions to help build your letter.

Letters of reference are like literature that can be analyzed for style and content. Administrators who read many reference letters—as well as write them—know what to look for and can easily differentiate the stronger ones.

Knowing what makes a good reference letter and providing the detail to help a reference write a compelling letter about you are important tactical steps to securing a teaching position. Be selective of who you ask and give them material to ease the writing process.

Types of Reference Letters

Some reference letters are general and applicable to any job scenario; others are targeted and specific. The first can be used for any school and any context; the latter, for one only.

If you are going to ask someone to take the time to generate a well-thought-out and well-written reference letter, you will want to keep this one to use again and again in your application process until you secure a teaching position. Letters of reference should always be of this nature, as you will be applying to multiple positions and cannot ask someone to write you a dozen separate letters. Leave the targeted and specific references for that dream job.

Reference Letter Contents Sheet

In providing the reference with a completed contents sheet, you increase the chances that the reference letter will reflect who you are and how you want to be perceived by administrators.

Because the general reference letter is meant to be used repeatedly and not for one particular institution, it should be broader and have more general appeal. Identifying this to your reference is instructive to her writing your letter. Include the following:

- why you want to teach (one specific overarching goal)
- what makes you an effective teacher (e.g., share three specific character traits)
- why you want to teach a particular grade level or subject (give a brief explanation)
- what your long-term professional goal is (share one)

Because the specific reference letter targets a specific school, detail is required. Include the following:

- position sought
- name of school or school districts

- primary contact information (e.g., address of school)
- primary contact person (include name, position, and e-mail address)
- timeline for submission (e.g., date application is due)
- brief details about the school (e.g., nondenominational, boarding school, Montessori)
- what appeals to you about the school (e.g., the neighborhood, the students, the faculty)
- why you want to teach there (e.g., specific subject, grade, geographical location)
- why you are suited for a position there (e.g., your credentials, your experience)

Strategies for Getting First-Rate References

1. **Build Relationships.** Your primary motive in getting a reference is to build relationships with key professionals. Get to know your professors, your principals, your colleagues, and anyone who is influential. This isn't about being nice in order to use someone; it is about building contacts and relationships with key people that you will keep for a long time. If they end up serving as your references, great. If they end up getting you a job, all the better.

2. **Identify Credible Sources.** Choose carefully and deliberately who you ask to serve as a reference. From within your placements, choose a principal, vice principal, or a supervising teacher. From your graduate work, choose a professor or course instructor. From past employment or volunteer work, choose your boss or supervisor. But don't ask everyone. A person who is asked to be your reference is honored with the opportunity; if everyone is asked, it is a chore.

3. **Build a Portfolio of Reference Letters.** Seek references from diverse areas in order to give the broadest and most comprehensive scope of your talents and personality. Having a

few reference letters in your portfolio and a few references to call upon puts you in good stead for acquiring a position.

4. **Read Many Reference Letters.** Become familiar with the contents of exceptional reference letters. Read many of them and select from the best. Isolate the characteristics that make them outstanding. Would someone write this about you?

5. **Write Your Own Reference Letter.** Put yourself in the position of your reference. What would *you* say about *you*? How would *you* promote your best qualities and best talents? If you know what makes a superb reference letter, if you know what your most endearing qualities are and what your greatest talents are, then you should be able to compose a persuasive reference letter that lands you the position. In your contents page to your reference, address some of these same points.

6. **Share Your Portfolio.** Prepare a brief portfolio of yourself to share with prospective references. Hand them your reference letter contents sheet along with your professional goals, personal statement, teaching philosophy, résumé, and cover letter. Make their task easier by highlighting aspects of your portfolio. Who knows? This reference may very well land you an unexpected position.

Next Steps

The paperwork is prepared, and your portfolio is complete. The next step is to orient yourself around the interview. What are the different types? What are the different stages? What questions are asked? What are the most effective strategies for a successful interview?

In the next section, we will look at all the details of a typical interview and how to prepare effectively so that you achieve the position. When the interview takes place, you are ready to ace it.

PART 3

Your Professional Interview

CHAPTER 6

Preparing for the Interview

Purpose

The purpose of the teacher interview is for the employer to determine whether the candidate is suitable for the job. Reaching this stage means you have done all the right things to appeal to the school administrators. Now it is time to persuade the employers in person that you are the only candidate for this position.

Recap

In your professional goals, you outlined your short- to long-term vision as an educator. In your personal statement, you identified many of your strongest traits, values, experiences, and skills. In your teaching philosophy, you expressed your attitudes and beliefs about teaching and learning, students, parents, and administrators, as well as envisioned your ideal classroom. You brought all of these notions into a well-crafted résumé and cover letter and also aligned your social media.

Now it is time to prepare for the interview.

Effective Interview Techniques

Many of these techniques seem obvious. But you would be surprised at how many times someone has walked through the door, having prepared for weeks, and blown the interview simply because he or she didn't present themselves professionally in appearance, behavior, or mannerisms. Consider the following more of a list of *best practices* in interview-taking skills.

Appearance

1. **Dress professionally.** It is better to err on the side of caution and use a very conservative, professional look rather than go in with casual or bold attire. If hired, you will be representing the school, and how you dress will not only reflect what the school values but will also influence the way students perceive you. Administrators are looking for professionalism in their teachers.

2. **Avoid scents.** Some people are quite sensitive to perfumes and colognes and can be turned off by a candidate if he or she is heavily scented. Some institutions even post *scent-free* signs around their buildings.

Behavior

1. **Arrive early.** Fifteen minutes before the actual interview time is a standard rule.

2. **Be cordial. Be grateful. Be polite.** First impressions are dealmakers.

3. **Be prepared.** Bring copies of your portfolio to distribute, if and when appropriate.

Speaking Mannerisms

1. **Maintain focus.** The flow of the interview can be fairly fast as the panelists rush through their prepared list of questions eager to hear your responses. But it could equally be on the slower side wherein fewer questions are asked and greater attention is given to how you answer rather than what you answer.

2. **Listen attentively. Ask for clarification.** Be sure you understand what is being asked of you. When uncertain, ask to rephrase it.

3. **Consider the subtext.** Why are they asking those particular questions? What underlying messages are they communicating?

4. **Speak clearly.** Use a clear, articulate voice in responses and ensure that each panelist hears you.

5. **Consider your tone.** Use an engaging and inviting tone. What tone suggests to you that a prospective employer would be interested in you? Confident? Polite? Respectful? Passionate? Eager? How do you want to present yourself?

6. **Avoid interjections, distracting mannerisms, and interrupting.** Be prepared and practice your responses. Avoid using *umms* and *uhhs* to fill the time, distracting hand gestures, and interrupting the questioner.

Facial Expressions and Body Language

1. **Maintain eye contact.** Ensure you are maintaining appropriate eye contact with the person asking the question but also with the other panelists. Regardless of who asks the question, all of the panelists are interviewing you.

2. **Body posture.** Maintain an actively engaged body posture by sitting straight up in your seat or leaning forward slightly; leaning back or crossing your arms suggests disinterest and disengagement.

Responses

1. **Balance speaking time.** Keep in mind that just because you are being interviewed does not mean that you are required to do all of the talking. It is realistic to expect speaking time to be

in the neighborhood of 30–40 percent interviewer and 60–70 percent interviewee.

2. **Give detailed responses.** Some questions are fairly open-ended and require detailed responses. These questions are opportunities for the panelists to hear you showcase what you know and for you to elaborate on experiences you have had. Treat them as chances to convince the panelists of your competencies.

3. **Be concise.** Some questions call for you to be succinct in your responses, sometimes in a few words or one sentence. Become familiar with recognizing these more closed-type questions. Clear, direct answers prevail.

4. **Use education terminology.** A teacher who knows the jargon and can express it appropriately in an interview appears to understand the language of education well and suggests an academic nature.

5. **Share educational theory.** At times, administrators want to know what you know about educational theory. Some questions require you to provide support for your points. Citing educators or strategies may be fitting.

6. **Provide practical applications.** Sometimes administrators want to hear how you can employ a theory in practice. How would you?

7. **Use formal language.** Although an interview is a dialogue, the tone should not be conversational; use formal language.

8. **Reference a person.** Mention a colleague or administrator that you know who works at the school and who can vouch for you. This is an easy way to present a reference.

9. **Reference an experience.** Experience is a significant teacher, and panelists want to know what you have learned from your experiences.

10. **Share an anecdote or tell a story.** People are drawn to stories and storytellers. Develop a few anecdotes that succinctly capture an experience you have had and that can demonstrate the learning you have gained. When appropriate, share a story that highlights a lesson learned about teaching. Simple and short anecdotes are memorable.

11. **Paint a vivid picture.** This strategy works best for situating the panelists in your ideal classroom. Give them a vivid image of what your classroom would look like. What would be on the walls? How would the desks be aligned? Where would students sit? How would the space be used? Add to this picture. How would students behave? How would they interact with you? What would they say? Use rich imagery and appeal to various senses.

12. **Anticipate questions.** Interviews have a natural order and flow that committees have practiced and streamlined for effectiveness and efficiency. Anticipate the kinds of questions and their order so that your responses are at the ready for delivery. In the final chapter of this work, we will look at the flow of the interview and the commonly asked questions.

13. **Be authentic.** Invariably, trust and honesty emerge when you are comfortable with people. If you find yourself opening up and sharing experiences, then you may just be building the kind of rapport that will get you hired.

Reading the Signs

People reveal a lot about themselves through their word choice, their tone of voice, their facial expressions, and their body language. Some people are very skilled at controlling their emotions and can present themselves in a way that leaves uncertainty as to what they are feeling. Others are very emotive, and their feelings are easily revealed.

Gauging the interview as it progresses helps you determine whether things are going well or whether you need to take a different tack—you might need to check what you are saying, change your style, or shift your approach.

Become adept at recognizing the signs.

1. **Reading eye contact.** Are the interviewers maintaining eye contact with you? Are they looking off in the distance or looking excessively at their notes? Too little eye contact suggests little engagement and little persuasion.

2. **Reading facial expressions.** Do your responses elicit positive, engaged emotions? Do the panelists appear eager to hear what you have to say? What are their facial expressions revealing? Are their eyes wide open and embracing your responses? Are their smiles? Facial expressions that are engaged tend to express the same emotions you are showing.

3. **Reading body language.** Are panelists sitting forward with body posture open and accepting? Are they leaning back, arms folded, and body closed?

4. **Listening for word choice.** If interviewers are following a scripted list of questions, then this may be harder to detect. Is she using what appears to be inviting language and more open-ended questions to solicit more dialogue from you or are the questions tending to be closed and your speaking amount significantly reduced?

5. **Identifying tone.** What tone of voice does the interviewer have? Is it curt? Does it suggest disinterest or boredom? Interviewers who have disengaged from the interview can change their tone from excited to stale or routine and appear unempathetic.

Redirecting the Interview

If you notice these signs during the interview, you will need to act quickly to recover the promise these committee members saw in you when they decided to meet you in person. Ingratiating yourself to each person is a must. How do you go about building rapport with each person? How do you get the panelists to see you as the ideal person for this position?

The more you can simulate an interview as you prepare for it, the better you can manage it when it happens, and the less likelihood of being caught in a position where you need to work harder to get the committee's approval.

Great Interviews

The best interviews are those that are successful on three fronts: the interviewer, interviewee, and the interview itself.

From the interviewer's perspective, the panelists managed to ask questions they prepared, heard answers they were looking for, and confirmed your general fit for the school. They developed confidence and comfort in your knowledge, skills, and personality and feel that you are a worthy candidate for this teaching position.

From the interviewee perspective, you managed to engage the committee members quite comfortably. You listened attentively to the questions and responded with answers that pleased the panel. You made a connection with each panelist, developed rapport, and built trust. You maintained professional composure and demonstrated integrity.

The ideal interview is well structured and paced perfectly. It allows the committee to ask all of its questions and the candidate to answer them thoroughly. The interviewers and candidate settle into a rhythm where there is a smooth flow and comfortable exchange of ideas. There is a great synthesis between all personalities in the room. An observer from a distance witnesses vocal tone, facial expressions, and body language become increasingly similar between the committee and the candidate as rapport develops. The chemistry in the room is strong. Expressions soften. Smiles form. And an overwhelming feeling of contentedness emerges.

Perfect interviews leave the committee members eager to hire the candidate, and the candidate is elated with the success of the interview.

But perfect interviews are rare. Developing strong chemistry on both sides of the table is difficult to do. The panelists need to *feel* that the candidate is the ideal person for the school, and the candidate needs to feel that the school is the *right place* to work. This is a challenging task. Despite the committee members having spent months weeding through handfuls of résumés looking for the best and the teacher candidate having taken an equal amount of time preparing all of the necessary documentation and practicing for the interview, it all comes down to this one forty-five-minute moment. Whatever happens in the interview is conclusive. The committee loves the candidate and is prepared to make an offer, or not. And the candidate loves the school and is excited about the prospect to work there, or not.

The Interviewer—A Different Perspective

For some time, we have been addressing what *you* would be doing during an interview. It is time to consider a different perspective. What is the *interviewer* doing?

Interviews are flawed. Many compromises are made that influence the final outcome. Some are the result of circumstance; others are the result of the parties involved. Recognizing the impact each side has allows for the candidate to prepare more effectively.

Interview Compromises

The following is a hypothetical scenario. Situate yourself as the candidate. Consider each compromise. What do you do? How do you handle each?

The department head, vice principal, and principal have previously met to discuss you as a potential employee at their school. They have reviewed your application and portfolio and have been very impressed with your credentials, your experience, and your personal character traits, and now they want to meet you. They are implementing new curriculum and want a fresh approach. You hold great promise. They look to you for your motivation, your passion, and your understanding of the latest theories in education. They anticipate your willingness to implement innovative teaching practices that will revitalize a somewhat stagnant school environment. They expect great things from you.

But first, you have to prove yourself in the interview. You have to persuade the panel that you are the ideal candidate they have envisioned. They know the virtual you, a persona crafted for the application and portfolio you have submitted. But what are you *really* like?

The interviewing panel is discriminating. Either you confirm their belief in you or you raise doubt. Poor hiring decisions are time-consuming. So administrators are going to be cautious, listening, watching, and wondering. Are you the right one?

Interviewers need to do their job well and in the best interests of the school. A poor decision in hiring could be detrimental to the school environment and very costly over the course of the year or years. While the purpose of an interview isn't to *catch you off guard*, the committee members will be discriminating about every aspect: your dress, your posture, your eye contact, your facial expressions, your body language, and, of course, your responses.

Time is a significant factor. Forty-five minutes isn't a lot of time to get to know the real you. However, that is all the time you have. So the interviewers come prepared with a list of questions from a broad range of categories and hope to get through the complete list. This is the ideal situation. If each question can be asked and thoroughly answered, then the interviewers stand a chance of having a fuller picture of you. But it is unrealistic to presume that all questions can be given the treatment they deserve. This is compromise number one. Which questions are left unasked? How do the panelists determine which to sacrifice? What if it was one of those questions that could have sealed the deal for you? The interview has not yet begun, and a compromise has already been made.

So the interview begins, and the first question is asked. You provide your first response, and the interviewers get the first real sense of who you are. Immediately, they begin to judge you. Are you articulate? Personable? Detailed? Are you confident? Are you competent? Do you have what it takes to be a teacher at their school?

A second question is asked. And then a third. And a fourth. The vice principal makes very brief notes. Compromise number two. What is she writing? You gave a very detailed response. How could she have possibly recorded your whole thought in the brief scratching on paper? What *has* she recorded? This creates a level of uncertainty.

The department head listens carefully to your responses but chooses *not* to make any notes. Why not? Why is *he* not recording any of your answers? How can he possibly remember what you are saying? Compromise number three.

The interview continues, and the vice principal decides to go off script. There are questions on the page before her, but she asks an entirely different one, one not previously planned. Why does she choose to ask you this question? Did the other candidates get this same question? Why are you being asked this in particular? Compromise four.

Of course, interviews are organic processes in which there is a dynamic give and take between the panelists and candidate. But this process is also limited to a brief moment in time. The interviewers cannot communicate with each other. What is each thinking? Often, interviewers who work closely together get very comfortable with each other's style and can read each other's expressions and tone of voice and can tell what the other is thinking. But this isn't always the case. How does each panelist's nonverbal response impact the way the interview progresses? Compromise five.

The principal is interrupted and has to excuse herself ten minutes before the interview is over. Compromise six.

Alarmed? Don't be. The purpose of this little scenario is to emphasize that there is no ideal interview. Every interview by its very nature is organic and flawed. Counting on it and being prepared for the unexpected will build your interview-taking skills.

Strategies to Mastering the Interview

As with most endeavors, the more you do something, the better you get at it—and there is no difference with the interview. The more you practice, the stronger your responses, the better your delivery, and the more persuasive you become.

Consider the learning continuum. Where do you rate yourself in overall interview skills? Which level are you at: beginning, developing, proficient, or mastery?

Understand the Types of Questions. Questions can be open-ended or close-ended. The former allow you to elaborate considerably.

Interviewers are looking for thorough and detailed responses. The latter are limiting in scope and call for you to be concise. For instance, *tell us a little about yourself* versus *where did you complete your practicum?*

Questions can also be of the theoretical, the practical, or the scenario kind. The first tests your knowledge of teaching practices and theory, the second asks what you have done and how you have done it, and the third challenges you to consider what you would do under certain circumstances. For instance:

Theoretical: What do you know of brain-based theory?

Practical: How would you go about using Backward Design in your practice?

Scenario: How would you handle a parent who was upset with the way you treated her child?

Understand the Areas of Questioning. There are many areas of questioning but a limited amount of interviewing time. Sometimes panelists only manage to ask a couple of questions from each area. Preparation for all areas ensures greater confidence and a stronger performance.

Write Out Your Responses. Take the time to write out your answers. Share and discuss these with your colleagues, teachers, or mentors. Refine your answers and practice delivering them until you are comfortable with them. Responses should be strong, clear, and direct. They should be fluid and somewhat organic. Memorized responses may work against you while practiced ones help you deliver off script comfortably.

Record Your Voice. Record yourself delivering your responses and listen to your voice. How do you sound? What is your tone? Are you *confident*? Do you sound *competent*? Do you hear yourself pausing frequently or using "umm" or "uhh"?

Video Record Yourself. Video record yourself and watch your eye contact, facial expressions, and body language as you deliver your responses. What are these revealing about you? Do you present yourself professionally, engaged, or self-assured?

Practice with Others. Practicing with others is a great way to get a more objective perspective on your method of delivery, as others may notice nuances in your style that you don't catch.

Get Professional Coaching. Coaches trained in interviewing strategies—and who don't know you—can probably give you the most objective feedback without fear of harming a close relationship.

Be the Interviewer. Change roles. Interview a colleague of yours. Assess her responses, presentation style, and body language. How does it feel? Do you get a sense of what panelists are looking for?

Mastering the Interview. You know you are prepared for the interview when responses come easily to you, when you light up with a smile as you are asked a question, and when you find it easy to engage with the questioner.

Witnessing an excellent interviewee is like watching a master at work with her craft. She easily connects with the panelists, making light conversation before the interview formally begins. She is kind and cordial, listens carefully, is genuine in her responses, and reveals compassion for children. She dresses professionally, is engaging in her tone of voice, receptive to feedback, and an overall delight.

This is the kind of person you would find building connections with students, getting them to trust her, developing their comfort with risk-taking, eager to achieve their best, and wanting to share in their accomplishments. This is also the kind of person you would find socializing with the parents and building supports with them to help their children.

Building Rapport and Developing Trust

Your task in the interview is to convince the panelists that you are the most desirable candidate; theirs is to determine if you are the right *fit* for the school. Can they trust that you have the students' best interests at heart?

Will you address the needs of the individual student? Do you know your subject matter? Do you have effective teaching strategies? Will you be professional in your conduct with students, parents, and administrators? Are you a team player? And so on.

No matter how well you prepare for each component, your primary task is to build rapport with each panelist and develop their trust. If you can make a connection with each person, then you come closer to persuading them that you are the best option available.

Next Steps

The next chapter is a simulation of a typical interview process from the application through to the offer and traces each of the stages, outlining strategies for achieving success at every step.

Interview Stages

Purpose

The interview process varies from school to school, but there are a few common stages that institutions rely on that have proven to be efficient and effective. The whole process may last days or weeks depending on the lead-up time to the position's availability as well as the school's needs. It begins with the phone screening, moves to the interview, then with reference checking, followed by a second round, and then ending with the offer. At any moment, the school will determine whether the candidate moves on to the next stage or not. It is a *sudden death* game.

Having conducted many interviews, I have witnessed what great candidates do during the whole process. Memorable moments leave lasting impressions. The best strategies are outlined below.

Step 1: Screening by Phone

Hiring is very time-consuming. Processes that increase efficiency save time and relieve the employer of additional burdens. Filtering programs enable the employer to short-list hundreds of applicants to a small handful of promising ones. Human resource personnel or assistants to principals read through this handful looking for key terms that capture their attention and suggest compatibility with the school.

At this stage, employers have framed an image of the candidate based on the profile. Now they want to hear what this virtual person sounds like.

A typical phone screening goes like this. An assistant or a human resource person—not necessarily the person directly responsible for hiring—calls the candidate. The call lasts no more than five to ten minutes. There is a brief introduction followed by a few questions. Often, the caller addresses points already covered in the résumé.

This type of call serves multiple purposes: the caller is listening for how you communicate, verifying what you have done, and wondering how much you want this position, among other things. Treat this call like an official interview. Employers have read your résumé and cover letter and might know the answers to the questions they are asking. Their objective is not to interview you over the phone but to determine whether it is worth investing time to interview you in person.

How you respond, of course, is common sense: answer the phone with a polite, confident, and assertive voice; declare affirmatively your application and interest in the position; listen attentively for the questions asked; and respond concisely and positively. The caller will probably want to confirm your educational background, your experiences, and your availability for the position. He will probably want to identify qualities about you that don't appear on your application.

You will give away many secrets about yourself, secrets you might not be aware that ultimately decide your fate with this position. Your tone, your clarity of voice, your confidence in your responses, and your attention to detail all implicate you and will lead the caller to make a judgment about your compatibility with the school.

By the time the phone call ends, the caller will have already made a decision about you and will be reporting that decision to the interviewing committee. There will be a clear *yes* or *no* about you as a prospective employee. If it is a *no*, chances are the caller did not confirm an interview time with you. If it is a *yes*, you will be given an interview time. Keep in mind, however, that *yeses* are just *maybes* in disguise. Focus your efforts on preparing for the interview.

Effective Screen Calling Strategies

A few small steps can dramatically increase your chances in the screening:

1. **Prepare for the call.** Anticipate this screening and prepare as if it is your *only* interview. Have your portfolio ready to reference if necessary.

2. **Expect the caller to be the final decision maker.** It is hard to gauge the caller's role in the decision-making process. Is this person an administrative assistant who is simply conducting a background check on your credentials appearing on your résumé? Or is this person part of the final interviewing panel with a significant stake in the decision to hire? Expect the latter and raise your level of preparation.

3. **Present yourself professionally.** Balance the more conversational nature of the phone call with the professional nature of an interview. You might find you begin with common language but end up using educational or specialty terminology.

4. **State something enduring about yourself.** Make a special point of highlighting something you did not include in your résumé or cover letter that piques the caller's interest and further identifies you as a potential candidate worthy of greater investment of time and resources.

5. **Leave the caller wanting more.** Highlight something about the school that you found particularly interesting. This lets the caller know that you have done your research. It is impressive, and *impressive* is what you want the caller to be thinking.

A successful screening results in a scheduled interview time. You have positioned yourself well, captured the caller's attention, and secured a formal meeting time. Now the major work begins.

Step 2: The Interview

The initial interview is often conducted by human resources personnel, teachers, department heads, or vice principals and rarely includes the person who will ultimately make the decision to hire. This stage serves as an opportunity for middle management to further screen candidates and short-list to a very few who will return for a second round.

This stage has various components that all offer opportunity for advancement along the hiring continuum. It begins with the gatekeeper, proceeds with the transfer to the meeting location, follows with the formal interview, then the transfer back to the gatekeeper, and ends with the departure from the building. The formal interview itself also has key components, including the arrival, the transition, the questioning, the turn, the benefits, and the wrap-up.

Each of these stages offers opportunities to make a positive impression. The more positive impressions you make, the greater the chances of securing the position. Preparing effectively will do much to persuade all involved that you are the worthiest candidate.

But all of this does not begin on the day of the interview; rather, twenty-four hours prior. Before you get to the interview, scope out the terrain. Take a drive to the school at the appointed hour one day in advance to judge the amount of time it will take you to get there as well as to determine where you will park. The day of the interview isn't a time to arrive late or flustered because you got caught in traffic or could not find a parking spot. Adjust your time as necessary.

Expect the whole process to last from one to two hours of your meeting time. Be sure not to schedule any other appointment too proximal to this time.

You will be checking in with the gatekeeper who will be expecting your early arrival.

Effective Initial Interview Strategies:

1. **Respect the fifteen-minute rule.** Check in at reception no later than fifteen minutes prior to your interview time.
2. **Embrace the one-chance approach.** Make this interview count as if it is the *only* chance you have of getting this job.
3. **Every personal interaction *is* an interview.** Every person you meet on this day is vital to your getting hired. Treat each person as if he or she is on the hiring committee and judging your candidacy for the position. Every word and every action counts.

Part One: The Gatekeeper

Your interview begins the moment you introduce yourself to the gatekeeper. He or she may make a judgment call about your fit for the school and pass it on to the key people, solicited or unsolicited.

In addition to the same strategies used in the screening interview, add the following:

1. **Record names.** When greeting the receptionist, be sure to listen attentively to the names of the interview panelists he or she shares with you as well as his or her own name. If he or she does not share these, ask for them. Record these as you wait.

2. **Leave a lasting impression.** Whether or not the receptionist shares anything with the interviewing team, this moment serves as an opportunity to present yourself as personable and professional. Saying, doing, or asking something that piques the interest of the receptionist can help you. Make *saying* or *doing* count in your favor.

3. **Develop a sense of the school culture.** Use the waiting time as an opportunity to research the culture of the school. Record things that you observe about the school, the community, the students, or the teachers. Collect a newsletter or other school pamphlets that are displayed. These might become helpful immediately in the interview or in the days to follow.

Part Two: The Transfer to the Interview Location

Someone will escort you to the meeting location. This person may or may not be on the interview panel. As with the gatekeeper, the same effective strategies apply. In addition, consider the following:

1. **Comment on the educational program.** Take note of what you see in the hallways, on the walls, or in the classrooms as you are led along the way. Make positive, engaging comments about what you see that reveal your understanding of that learning strategy or educational program.

2. **Reference what you know of the school.** Leave this person feeling that you have done your homework researching the

school and that you have had experience with these teaching methodologies finding significance and success in their implementation.

In the few moments it takes to arrive in the meeting room, you will have already left an impression with the person escorting you. Make it positive and endearing. If you simply walk quietly down the hallway, that person will question your sociable nature and wonder about your interpersonal skills.

Part Three: The Initial Interview

The Arrival

Event: You'll meet two or three people, each of whom may have conducted many interviews and be very practiced in this process. They will expect a certain standard and protocol. Count on it. But don't be surprised if someone or more than one are new themselves to the process. After all, everyone has to start sometime.

Purpose: At this stage, the panel is attempting to *size you up*. They are listening to your communication skills, watching your social interactions, and seeing how well you understand people and how well you present yourself. They want to know how you hold yourself and what your facial expressions and body language communicate. *Are you approachable? Will students understand you? Will they show immediate respect for you as the authority in the classroom? How will parents perceive you?*

Effective Strategies: Be direct with your eye contact, firm with your handshake, and pleasant with your word choice. Listen carefully to each name as people introduce themselves. Repeat their first name and comfortably state yours with a proper greeting like "It's a pleasure to meet you." Be clear and confident.

The Transition

Event: You will be asked to take a seat as they signal a place for you. This may be around a table, on a couch, or at a desk. There will be small talk about the weather or traffic.

Purpose: This is an important moment to break the tension. The employer wants to set you at ease so that you are comfortable with the environment and the people.

Effective Strategies: Scope the room and determine where each person will sit. It should be obvious to you, but it isn't always. Only take a seat when you are directed to and engage in discussion as appropriate.

The Formal Interview

Event: You will be asked a series of questions from a variety of areas to test your knowledge, your experience, your communication skills, and a host of other areas—see all seventeen in the next chapter.

Purpose: The panelists will make critical judgment calls about you. They will be judging your level of competence to manage a classroom, cope with the demands of lesson planning, keep up with assessments and evaluations, work well with the team, and have good rapport with students, faculty, and parents.

Effective Strategies: Approach this interview with practiced skill at delivering your responses. Preplanned and studied responses that you can deliver almost without fail in a very confident, clear, and articulate manner demonstrate your preparedness and your professionalism. The final chapter in this book will prepare you considerably for every possible question.

The Turn

Event: Toward the end of the interview, someone on the panel will suggest that it is time to reverse the roles so that *you* have an opportunity to ask questions.

Purpose: This is a final transition moment in which the panelists once again want to set you at ease so that you can relax for a moment after what might be considered a grueling series of questions. The panelists don't expect to learn anything from you at this time, but this is when you reveal something that is vital to their decision making.

Effective Strategies: Take this as an opportunity to strengthen your position by asking clearly planned questions about their school or strategic plan. Consider highlighting an accomplishment of yours that aligns with their school. For instance, "When I was grading AP exams in English, I developed a technique to help me grade them. I noticed your students take AP English Language. Is the strategic plan to increase participation? Or to increase performance?" This might lead the panelists to reveal aspects of their own strategic plan, but more importantly, will serve you well in piquing their interest and further confirming your candidacy. The simple rule: make whatever you ask critical to your success.

The Benefits Plan

Event: This may or may not take place in the initial interview, depending on the school and the committee's objectives. It comprises a brief summary of all the benefits they will offer you, if hired.

Purpose: It is important for them to identify the benefits package to you. They want you to be fully aware of what you are committing yourself to if you are offered a position. If the benefits package is appealing to you, then they can proceed with deciding further whether to pursue you. If it's not appealing to you, then the process ends, and they will know not to bother continuing to pursue you and save themselves a lot of time.

Effective Strategies: In preparation for the interview, you will have generated a list of typical benefits. Check each of these off mentally as you listen.

The Wrap-Up

Event: At this stage, the interview is just about over, and the panelists are getting up off their seats, thanking you for coming in, and ushering you to the door.

Purpose: They will be letting you know that they will be making a decision by a certain date and you will be contacted if you receive a second round call or make the cut.

Effective Strategies: This is the final moment you have in the initial interview to persuade the hiring committee of your candidacy. Having a closing comment or two prepared is appropriate. You could suggest that you look forward with hope to becoming a member of this team and that you are excited about the prospect of bringing on a specific initiative that aligns with the school.

Part Four: The Return to the Gatekeeper

You might be escorted back to reception or you might be directed there. If you are escorted, then a last opportunity exists for you to say something memorable and leave a lasting impression. Take advantage of the moment. This could include highlighting something discussed in the interview or something you saw along the way regarding the academic programs, the school culture, or the facilities.

Part Five: The Departure from the Building

Before leaving, gather up any final bit of information you can about the school and the people you met. Jotting notes will help tremendously in the follow-up moments. Record all of the details you can but especially the names of each person you met with. Before exiting the building, check with reception for the spelling of each person's name. Get their e-mail addresses if you can. Let the receptionist know that you will be sending them thank-you e-mails and ask which addresses would be best to send these to. Do so with the receptionist as well.

The initial interview is now over.

Part Six: The Follow-Up

The first day or two following the interview is critical to your success and comprises five important parts: note taking, thank-you e-mails, reference calls, reflection, mailed thank-you cards, and the follow-up call.

Note Taking

Record as many details as you can about the questions asked and the people you met. How well do you remember everything that you saw or that was said? Make notes on the school's mission, vision, strategic plan, students, parents, faculty, academic program, cocurricular offerings, overall school culture and community.

As well, it is important to understand each of the people you met and gauge what he or she is looking for in a candidate. Along the way, what did each reveal about themselves that you can address in an e-mail?

Thank-You E-mail

Later that day, send an individually addressed e-mail to each of the panelists as well as the gatekeeper. Recognize the value of their time and thank them for sharing some with you. Comment on one aspect of the school culture you found particularly poignant, differentiating them as an outstanding institution. End with a note of looking forward to the opportunity to meet again in the near future. Be sure to personalize each e-mail, acknowledging something different in each one.

Consider this: the panelists regroup after a grueling week of interviews. They have a lot to report on each candidate. When they get to you, they have e-mails to share. Each panelist notices that you personalized your e-mails, highlighting something unique and memorable about him or her. Which candidate do *you* think will be most remembered?

If you are not provided with each person's e-mail address, then send the message to the receptionist, and in the address window, record the person's name you want the message sent to.

Reference Checks

Without fail, contacting your references at this stage is a must. Notify them of the experience you have just had. Of course, you will want to let them know who will be calling and why. But above that, you want to provide your references with some important details: what kinds of questions were asked, what did these suggest they are looking for in a new hire, what salient points about the school or school community are important for the reference to know?

If the reference is to support you in getting a job, then providing details about the school and its personnel acts as leverage. When the reference is contacted, he can elaborate specifically on your traits and experiences that will lead to landing you the position. Tailored responses for each school are tantamount to well-aimed and well-directed efforts.

There is so much you could concentrate on in your follow-up discussions with your references. For those you are much closer to, you could probably give a thorough and detailed walk through of the whole process. But this might not always be the case with your references. Some, you might only know professionally and want to maintain a much briefer and more focused follow-up conversation. In either case, covering the following three areas of the interview is fitting: the people, the school, and the culture.

Letting your references know the names of the people you met and providing a few brief character points is helpful to understanding who and what they are looking for in a new hire.

Reflection

The bulk of the work is done. Now it is time for serious reflection. Reflect objectively on the people you met, the school you saw, and the way the interview progressed. Is it a place you want to work at in the immediate future? What about five or ten years from now? Do you still see yourself working there and prospering? What do you think about the people you met? Could you work closely with them? Will they give you autonomy in the classroom and respect your independence as a teacher? Will they support your initiatives? Do you see yourself becoming a better educator in this school culture?

Eagerly saying yes to an offer because of the promise of full-time work might be a good short-term decision but not necessarily the best for a long-term commitment.

Formal Thank-You Cards

Despite having already sent an e-mail the day of the interview, a formal thank-you card arriving two or three days later in the mail does wonders for the panelists in determining who to pursue further. After all, they probably completed a series of interviews that day, or over multiple days, or even weeks. Your e-mail kept them thinking of you, and your card reminds them of you again.

Assessing and evaluating the merits of each candidate is not an easy task for the committee. They meet many people, see them for less than an hour, and then have to make a decision for the future of the school based on these glimpses. Help the panelists. Give them a reason to offer you the job.

As with the thank-you e-mail, the formal thank-you card follows the same format. Remember, you are not trying to sell yourself. Your best bet for success is respect, acknowledgment, and gratitude.

Follow-Up Call

An interview committee never wants to feel pushed into making a decision; treat follow-up phone calls with caution. Determining the appropriate time to make this call is dependent on the timeline the school posted or shared with you regarding next steps. If there is ample time, weeks or months before the school year begins, then waiting a week or two is appropriate. If the job is to begin the following month, then a few days later or early the following week seems called for. This is something that needs to be gauged accordingly.

The purpose of the follow-up phone call is simply to ask if there has been any progress made in the process. What is the best way you can think to address this?

Behind the Scenes: What Happens Following the Initial Interview

Before looking at the second round, it is important to understand what happens following the initial interview from the perspective of the hiring committee.

Phone Screening Impressions

In the initial short-listing phase and before the phone screening, school personnel flagged your application because it intrigued them. They made a few notes, highlighting aspects of your character or work experiences or personal interests. This short-listing allowed the school to narrow the scope of applicants to a handful of promising ones who share some alignment with the school's mission, vision, strategic plan, or culture. And you made the cut.

Behind the scenes, what you don't know has happened is that there has already been much talk about you and your candidacy for the position. It began at this short-listing stage. The interviewing committee sat around a table discussing you, your résumé, and your cover letter. They talked about your experiences, your education, and your character. They asked many questions about you like: *Why did he get that undergraduate degree? Why did she decide to attend that teacher's college program? Why did he hold those part-time jobs?*

Many questions were asked and many impressions made. Your reputation, essentially, was forming. The person making the screening phone call was directed with a series of questions. Some were to confirm what you communicated in your application, others to clarify your personal character traits.

The committee reviewed their questions in conjunction with those answers you gave. At this point in the whole process, the committee is now attempting to understand your character. *Are you true to what you communicated in your portfolio?*

Some of their concerns are assuaged through your responses. Some, however, come not from the content of your answers but from your tone and delivery style. How you speak is often more important at this stage than what you speak. Regardless of whether you have had excellent educational experience or teaching practice, if your tone is unsettling in the very brief phone call, then it raises concerns for the committee. *What'll happen during the school year? How will your tone unsettle students, faculty, or parents?* The committee will discuss this.

The committee now has a clearer picture. But many questions still need to be answered to further understand your character.

At this stage, some schools will generate a list of questions based on what came out of the phone screening. Other schools will work off the same questions they pose to everyone. Best practices suggest that an optimum balance of standard questions coupled with specific tailored questions generates the best results.

The Initial Interview Impressions

In forty-five minutes, an interviewing committee can size you up pretty accurately: the content of your responses, the detail you provided, your word choice, the tone you used, your eye contact, facial expressions, body language, and posture.

Whatever concerns the panelists had prior to your arrival should have been resolved with this interview. Following your visit—sometimes immediately after or in the next day or two—there will be a follow-up meeting of the committee. They will review your personality, your responses, and the impressions they had of you prior to meeting you and then following. The committee is essentially confirming that *who you say you are* and *how they perceive you* are one and the same.

Knowing yourself is crucial. This cannot be stated enough. Presenting yourself professionally *equally* in your portfolio and in person is paramount to your success.

If the interview in any way highlighted personal characteristics that differed from those communicated in the profile, then the committee will be suspect of you and probably not want to pursue you further—after all, the person on paper does not appear consistent with the person in real life.

If, on the other hand, paper and real life are consistent, then the panelists need to consider: *do we want this person or not?*

The committee will review their questions along with your answers. They will highlight memorable responses. They will note what you did not say. They will look at how clear and direct you were. They will look to where you placed most emphasis.

Consider two equal candidates both speaking on the subject of engaging student interest. The first shares strategies he has witnessed to be effective in the classroom. The second speaks of how he engages students to become passionate about a subject. Which do you think an interviewing panel would lean toward? What about how one spent much time reflecting on appropriate classroom management strategies and the discipline practices while the other focused on building rapport with students and getting them to understand their role as members of a group in a class? How would you choose?

Comparisons

A hiring committee might begin the search process with an ideal candidate in mind. They might consider what kind of educational experience the person has had, how many years, in which field, where, and when. They might consider the character traits they are looking for and what talents that person possesses. But in the end, the committee might not find this ideal candidate. What they might find instead are a few very promising candidates who are close to—but not exactly—hitting the mark. At this point, it is no longer about the ideal candidate but about the best person out of the bunch.

This is the comparison process. The committee begins weighing one person against the other, noting the qualities in one that the other does not possess. A mental *pros and cons* chart is drawn up for each candidate. Further questions arise as the committee differentiates each one and tries to come to terms with a ranking order of qualities and characteristics. Throughout this process, the committee realizes how certain questions were asked of one candidate that were not of another due to time. The whole process becomes a little more complex as the committee begins to realize that the closer they come to understanding each person, the more they are comparing apples to oranges: what one candidate brings to the table is highly beneficial to the school for certain reasons, and what another brings is likewise but for other reasons.

What the committee invariably has is a short list of highly qualified candidates with exceptional skills, talents, and passions who will all enhance the school community greatly—each in different ways. What the committee does not have is multiple job opportunities. The ranking of such high-quality candidates is a difficult dilemma.

The solution is twofold: the first is to call on the references to help differentiate each candidate; the second is to have a follow-up interview with more specific questions that will create a greater divide between *the best* candidate and *the second best*.

Reference Impressions

Reference checks are mandatory. Teachers work in the *vulnerable* sector. Schools would be remiss if they did not conduct thorough investigations of all promising candidates.

But every promising candidate has different references. How does a committee go about comparing each reference's responses when they appear to come from different sectors of society or from different levels of status within organizations? It's not as though each candidate has an equivalent number of references from equivalent sectors, with equivalent levels of responsibility to make a comparison *equivalent*.

References *are* necessary. There is no doubt. How they impact the process is both helpful and hindering. A reference can provide very glowing comments about you. But does that reference's character also require a reference? One reference may have only known you for three months but is a principal while another may have known you for many years as your supervisor in a nonteaching capacity. Which will the committee find most helpful? Which will the committee want to know more from?

The impressions committees get of you from your references are highly informative and paint a much more detailed picture. Your legitimacy might be won over entirely here. References can, effectively, get you the job.

Often, however, schools want to have a second round. They want to be able to see you again, recalling what they learned from the phone screening, what they saw in person, and then what they heard from your references. If you have made it to this round, you can picture the interview committee with a contented expression on their faces. They like what they see, are happy with what they have heard, and are hopeful that they will be making the right decision very soon.

Reference Questions:

Below are sample questions an interviewer would ask a reference.

- How long have you known the candidate? In what capacity?
- Tell me a little about your professional relationship with him.
- Tell me a little about his professional conduct.
- What three words would you use to describe her? Why?
- Can you share an anecdote or two that support who she is or how she behaves?
- Would you hire her?

However, this is quite a generic list. If you have made it this far, you are the best person for generating a list of questions references could be asked. The questions might be from the above list, but chances are they will also be highly personal and based on responses you gave in the interview. What questions do you think they will ask your references?

Step 3: The Follow-Up Interview

To recap, the initial interview has gone as planned: you prepared effectively for all areas of questioning; you answered each question appropriately; you demonstrated qualities of a personable and competent educator; you built rapport with the panelists; and you did all the right follow-up things to let the committee know you are the worthiest candidate for the teaching position.

Often at the end of the initial interview, a panelist will inform you of the next steps, along with a suggested timeline for filling the position. Some schools and school districts complete the reference check and end their hiring process. Others conduct a follow-up round.

This follow-up differs only slightly from the first and often includes a change in personnel, questions, length, format, and tone.

Personnel

Initial interviews are conducted by a variety of people and can include teachers, department heads, vice principals, or human resource personnel. This initial team is commissioned with completing a thorough investigation of each candidate. As a committee, they have completed a call screening, planned and conducted the first round, and followed up with reference checks, all the while reconvening to discuss the merits—and demerits—of each person. They are charged with all of the preliminary work prior to the second round. They have gathered a lot of evidence about a teacher's capacity and fit for the school and have probably whittled the original list down to one, two, or three highly promising candidates. It is time to take one last look at each possibility and complete one more final and thorough check. This interview is about selecting the *best* candidate from the best *candidates*.

Ultimately, the decision to hire rests not with the original members of the panel but someone of greater authority or responsibility. The original interviewing panel is dissolved and a new one formed. The constitution of this new group differs to include the person or people who will say *yay* or *nay* along with one or two members of the original group. Knowing the composition of this new committee better informs you so that you can plan your responses and engagement accordingly.

Questions

Second-round interviews rarely comprise the same questions asked in preliminary ones. After all, those initial questions were asked and answered; to ask them again is redundant. However, as there are new members on this panel, you might find some of the same questions but reworded slightly. Schools often tailor the second-round interview to the person. There might be some general questions, and there might be some highly personalized questions based on responses you gave in the first interview or from information gleaned from your references.

1. **Comparative.** This round is all about differentiating each candidate further so that the divide between the first, the second, and the third is increased dramatically. The questions asked are going to achieve the greatest distinction between each candidate.

2. **Scenario.** Given equal educational experience, teaching practicums, and professional and personable natures, candidates are hard to differentiate. Introduce very specific scenario questions to that school's culture, student body, or teaching faculty, and equally capable candidates suddenly become easy to differentiate—and this is what the panelists want. By figuring out how you will respond in a given situation that takes place at their school, they can resolve the differences between multiple candidates and choose the one with the best fit.

3. **Character.** The new addition to the committee does not know you, and despite how well the team has presented you, this person must still see and witness for herself what you are like. Questions of character in this round are crucial to confirming what the authority figure has already heard from the team. There should be no surprise at this point—only a confirmation of character and desire to get to know the interviewee further.

4. **Elaboration.** Initial rounds are often set up back-to-back over a series of days in which a committee might see a handful to a couple of dozen prospective teachers. Taking notes on each candidate and keeping them distinctly different in the interviewers' minds isn't as easy as it might appear. At times, notes are clear and legible and people clearly differentiated. At others, a dizzying array of notes shows conflicting or overlapping

thoughts and a muddying of people. Some questions in the follow-up might be repeat questions. The panelists might have noted something in a response you previously gave but would like you to provide more detail. This could include reasking the earlier question or simply asking a subset question that you can elaborate on.

Length

Second-round interviews rarely last the length of time of first-round interviews. Anticipate this one to be approximately thirty minutes but don't be surprised if it is longer. Sometimes it strictly confirms what the panel already knows about you and serves more as an unofficial acceptance of you as their new employee. But this is rare.

Format

A new committee composition and a second round suggest the format will also change—sometimes it does and sometimes it does not. Prepare as you did for the initial interview, considering you don't know the panel's motives until the interview begins, and even maybe until after it ends. Follow the same recommendations and strategies for a more confident outcome.

Tone

The most promising aspect of the follow-up interview is that you have intrigued the committee. How you handled the first round and what the references suggested about you persuaded people to invest more time in you. They like you. They see potential in you. They might already want you. The tone of this interview, from the perspective of the committee, therefore, will probably be less interrogative, skeptical, and probing and more comforting and heartwarming. You might find the panelists more at ease and maybe even less cautious or secretive. You might find yourself more relaxed, sharing more personal anecdotes, feeling less intimidated like you are in the hot seat.

But don't let your guard down. Do all the right things you did the first time around. Be clear, confident, pleasant, professional, and thorough. Continue to build rapport and develop relationships with each panelist, especially the newest members. Differentiate yourself further. Provide greater anecdotes that help the committee visualize you in the classroom. Review your interview strategies and master your delivery.

Step 4: The Offer

This step requires little direction or discussion. The purpose of this whole work is to get you the offer. Now make the decision. Take it or leave it.

Next Steps

The following chapter includes a thorough overview of each part of the interview as well as a comprehensive list of questions along with a detailed explanation of each section. Interviews are comprehensive. Preparing effectively for each type of question means you are ready for whichever they choose to ask you.

CHAPTER 8

Interview Questions

Purpose

The list below comprises a broad range of areas commonly questioned during interviews. Preparing for all areas ensures a stronger performance, a satisfied interview panel, and—if all goes well—a job prospect realized.

Your professional goals, your personal statement, your teaching philosophy, your résumé, your cover letter, and your professional brand are all instrumental in your preparation for the interview. Many of the responses you generated in previous chapters helped you compose these documents. These will all help you master the interview questions.

Series 1: Introductory Questions and Recent History

This is the *getting to know you* section of the interview in which the panelists ask general questions to break the ice and ease the tension. The purpose? To acclimatize you, make you feel comfortable, and to get you speaking about yourself in an easy, nonthreatening manner. The questions are simple, factual, and open-ended.

Although it is only the start of the interview, the panel is sizing you up. They are listening to how you express yourself and watching your facial expressions, eye contact, and body language. They are judging your style, mannerisms, professionalism, and the content of your responses. They are wondering how students will respond to you, how you will interact with colleagues, and how you will be perceived by parents. *What* you communicate and *how* you communicate it matter.

1. Tell us a bit about yourself.
2. What are you currently doing? How does this help you in your goal to become a teacher?
3. Why do you want to teach?
4. Why is teaching rewarding for you?
5. Have you had teaching experience before? As a student? As a teacher? Or substitute?

Series 2: Educational Experience

Rarely does this section get the attention it deserves. If compromises are made, this is the first section to go. Interviewers would rather ask more relevant questions impacting your teaching performance than questions regarding your educational training. Nevertheless, having prepared responses is advised.

There are two reasons for asking about your educational experience: the first is regarding your motive for becoming an educator, and the second is regarding your competence in the subject matter.

The first is an important question. Why have you become a teacher? Given your undergraduate degree, there are many jobs you could have pursued. Why teaching? Unfortunately, I've heard many people comment that teaching was their *fallback* career and many others talk about *summers off*—two points never to make in an interview.

The second reason is also important. How well do you know your subject matter? It might not be so significant if you are a generalist teaching grade-four math, science, social studies, and English. But it becomes increasingly more important if you are a high school teacher teaching calculus, biology, or computer science, for instance. Thorough application processes include a proficiency test in which you sit an exam to determine your capacity for teaching the subject. Some schools conduct the interview entirely in the target language you will teach—for instance, French. Others ask that you model a lesson before a single panelist or the entire committee.

As more teacher candidates enter the profession with a second undergraduate degree or postgraduate work—like a master's or PhD— the level of specialization in the higher disciplines rises. For a school, this could be a great opportunity with more talented professionals entering the field. However, it could also complicate matters. Having additional credentials might need to be defended. If this reflects you, the panel will want to know why you did not pursue the field of academia even further, enter the university profession, or enter a field more related to your specialty, rather than the teaching profession. Panelists might even view your application to this position as a step down from where you were and consider you *overqualified*.

Nevertheless, there are many schools with a strong international reputation, particularly high schools, that may be offering Advanced Placement courses or the International Baccalaureate program who will be specifically looking for highly qualified and talented educators to deliver university-level material to high school students. Schools such as these are quite a draw for teacher candidates with multiple degrees and should be of serious consideration if you fit this description.

In your preparation, think about your undergraduate degree and how it has shaped your decision to become a teacher. Consider your chosen field, your specialization, which courses most appealed to you and why, as well as what educational delivery methods helped you the most.

1. Why did you decide to pursue your undergraduate degree?
2. What did you find most rewarding about your undergraduate experiences?
3. Why did you decide not to continue pursuing that field and get a career in that industry?
4. Why did you choose to attend that university for your undergraduate degree?
5. Why did you choose to attend that university for your teacher's college certification?
6. Tell me about your favorite subjects while in teacher's college.
7. What activities did you take part in outside of your academic studies? (athletics, arts, service)

8. Why did you decide to major in preschool, primary, junior, intermediate, or senior education?

Series 3: Teaching and Practicum Experience

Recent graduates from teacher's college programs have learned a lot of theory and practiced multiple strategies in their practicum. Some of these experiences will have been very positive while others will have been less so. There will have been a lot of risk-taking, successes, and failures. The panelists want to know what worked, what didn't, and how you handled yourself when things did not work out the way you expected them to.

Panelists understand that it takes time to hone teaching skills—even educators with years of experience are continually challenged by new programs, delivery methods, and learning styles. Teachers are not expected to have all of the answers, but they are expected to understand what it takes to be effective. Candidates who present themselves as innovative in their methods and reflective in their practice are more likely to be effective in the classroom—correcting methods and redelivering until students master the concepts.

Prepare a few anecdotes. Think about the experiences you have had and develop a few brief stories about the process you followed in planning and delivering a lesson, checking for understanding and reteaching as needed. Highlight what you learned in these experiences and how you resolved to improve your practice.

As well, consider the following questions:

1. Describe your student teaching experiences.
2. What was most rewarding about your experiences?
3. What was your greatest challenge? How did you resolve it?
4. What was your working relationship with the associate teacher?
5. How did the students receive and respond to you?
6. How involved were you in communicating with parents?
7. Were you given complete independence in your practicum?
8. How did you go about planning lessons and units?
9. How did you assess and evaluate student performance?
10. What did you learn most from this experience?

Series 4: Philosophy of Teaching

Committees are looking for passionate educators who are effective in their practice. They are looking for confidence and competence. Teachers enter the profession filled with ambition, ready and engaged to put into practice all that they have learned in college.

Having completed a full year or two in your teacher certification program, you will have already formed many opinions and beliefs about teaching and learning. You will have heard from various professors and instructors on a host of issues and topics; visited multiple classrooms; witnessed multiple teachers and teaching styles; and practiced a variety yourself.

Your completed teaching philosophy will support your presentation as a competent, articulate, and determined educator. Panelists love to interview candidates who know themselves well and can respond to every question convincingly. For a panel, it inspires confidence in the candidate; for the candidate, it crystalizes the possibility.

Many teaching philosophy questions appeared in chapter 5. As you prepare for this section, review the responses you gave in your teaching philosophy.

1.   Why do you want to teach?
2.   Why do you think you would make an effective teacher?
3.   What do you find rewarding or fulfilling about teaching?
4.   What is your philosophy of teaching?
5.   What is your preferred grade level? Discipline? Why?
6.   Describe your ideal student.
7.   How would you design your classroom? Why?

Series 5: Teaching and Learning

Teaching is an evolving occupation. The profession is constantly changing as new material is learned about brain development, human behavior, student learning, and what methods of teaching are most effective.

Employers are looking for faculty who will embrace this dynamic. Teachers need to be students of education in order to be effective teachers.

Learners take initiative. They set goals, take risks, and grow from their experiences. A good teacher-learner models what students do on a daily basis. A good teacher-learner also empathizes with students, understanding what the learning process is and better judging student performance. A good teacher-learner is, herself, adaptable. She is willing to continually learn new material and apply it to her own teaching. She attends conferences and workshops, signs up for professional development courses, and upgrades her credentials. She visits colleagues' classrooms for ideas in designing ideal learning environments or to witness different approaches to teaching.

1. How do you keep current?
2. How do you innovate your practice and appeal to the changing needs of the students?
3. What teaching strategies do you employ in your daily lessons?
4. How do you ensure students have learned the material, or the skill, or completed the task properly?
5. How do you individualize instruction?
6. How do you differentiate instruction to meet the needs of the remedial student, the general student, and the enriched student?
7. How do you meet the needs of English language learners?
8. How do you meet the needs of students with differing learning abilities?
9. **Example**: Provide an example in which you remediated a student's learning. Was the process successful? How do you know?
10. **Example**: Provide an example in which you enriched a student's learning. How did you go about designing your plan? What did you learn from the experience?

Series 6: Curriculum Knowledge and Planning

Schools are looking for competence in curriculum knowledge and planning.

Understanding curriculum standards is necessary for effective planning. Knowledge of the subject matter is also important. A person hired to teach multiple subjects for which he has not majored puts him at a slight disadvantage to the person who knows her subjects and does not need to learn the material to plan effective lessons. Which would you hire?

Employers want to be assured that you *know* the subjects, that you plan effectively, and that you consider varying learning abilities. They expect that you apply best practices and that you build in opportunities for critical thinking, creative thinking, and problem solving.

The strongest of teachers have their curriculum planned out for the whole year with each unit set up to include the overall and specific objectives and the assessments that will best demonstrate student learning. They have lessons planned with consideration for their students' abilities, learning styles, prior knowledge, and interest. They have plans designed with holidays in mind and for the busy time periods within the year. They also have backup plans for moments that may disrupt their efforts. Effective teachers anticipate all this and plan accordingly.

But interviewing committees also know that new teachers to the profession may not have all of this knowledge or experience yet. An effective strategy for the new teacher in acing this section of the interview is curriculum review. Reading over the curriculum guides for the subjects and grades for which you are interviewing prepares you to deliver convincing responses. How well do you know the overall expectations? How well do you understand the sample units, tasks, and recommendations for assessment?

Consider the following:

1. How familiar are you with the curriculum guides for your preferred grade or subject?
2. What process do you follow when planning a lesson or unit? Is there a particular model that you have found effective?
3. When planning a lesson or unit, what do you take into consideration?
4. **Example**: Provide one successful lesson you planned. What steps did you take? How do you know you were successful in your planning? What are the indicators?

5. **Example**: Describe one lesson that didn't go as well as you intended. What didn't seem to work? How did you recover the lesson and ensure there was some success?

Series 7: Assessment and Evaluation

Great planners generate rich performance tasks and practical assessments. If you are an effective planner, then you consider assessments that will best demonstrate whether students have learned and achieved the expectations of the course.

Having a broad knowledge of assessment types as well as experience delivering these methods helps you become a stronger educator, as you will be able to anticipate which tasks are best suited for which lessons and units.

Teachers can get trapped easily. They settle for the same assessment forms repeatedly: for instance, the math teacher who only assesses with tests and quizzes or the English teacher who only assesses with paragraphs and essays. Although each of these assessment types is highly valuable, the trap is in refusing to go beyond these approaches and try something new, appealing to different learning styles or methods of expressing. Communication, for instance, can vary significantly in its level of sophistication. A formal analytic essay and a video are both worthy activities. There may be a greater demonstration of skill development and knowledge acquired putting together the video over the essay—and vice versa—depending on the expectations of the tasks.

Employers are looking for teachers who conscientiously choose assessments that best fit the expectations of the course and that engage students and motivate them to showcase their talents. How many different assessment types are you familiar with? How many have you used?

With assessment comes evaluation. What are the purposes of the tasks? What do you do once you have a host of assessments before you? How do you determine that students have achieved all of the course expectations? How do you evaluate them?

1. What do you believe the purpose of assessment and evaluation to be?

2. What forms of assessment would you use in a given subject and grade?
3. What types of diagnostic, formative, and summative assessment do you like to use? Why?
4. What kinds of assessments do you find most effective? Why?
5. What role do you see self-assessment and self-evaluation playing in student learning?

Series 8: Learning Environment

The personality of the teacher dictates the learning environment in the classroom. Despite there being possibly thirty students in the classroom offering thirty unique personality types ultimately influencing the learning environment, it is the teacher who sets the tone. He is the one that designs the space, creates the atmosphere, sets expectations high, motivates, fosters teamwork, empowers, builds confidence and self-esteem, and produces the setting for students to take risks, learn, and grow.

In their evaluation of you, a committee will consider your personality and how you will influence the learning environment.

What you say and how you say it will be projected by the panelists to your classroom. They will envision you speaking and presenting to the students and will wonder whether what you say and how you say it will engender a positive learning environment and whether students will be eager to learn. They will wonder whether students will show you respect and be led by you.

What do employers want to see in the classroom?

1. If you had the opportunity to design your ideal classroom, what would the physical space look like? Paint a picture for us of what we would see when walking into your classroom.
2. What furniture would you have in your classroom? How would it be laid out? Why?
3. What would appear on the walls?
4. What kind of atmosphere would you create in this ideal learning environment?
5. If we walked into your classroom, what would we see students doing? How would we see them behaving?

Series 9: Classroom Management

Classrooms demand management. Students need leadership to guide them to achieve success. Leading by example and developing opportunities for student leadership makes for much more effective teaching and learning experiences for all involved.

Employers want to know that the teacher-leader can model respect and responsibility and engender these in his students. Effective leaders have integrity.

Students mimic the behavior of the adults around them. If we set high expectations for ourselves, we do so for them naturally.

Interviewing committees need to know that there is structure in the classroom, that there is process, respect, management, and discipline.

1. How do you establish order and process in your classroom?
2. How does student leadership manifest in your classroom?
3. What strategies have you found effective in managing a classroom?
4. What techniques have you found effective in handling discipline?
5. **Scenario**: Two boys have been repeatedly fighting in your classroom, and while you've kindly asked them to stop, this behavior continues. What do you do?
6. **Scenario**: A student continues to challenge your authority in the class. She insists on making it difficult for you. How do you handle the situation?

Series 10: Students

Ultimately, teaching *is* about students. It is about getting them from point A at the beginning of the year to point B by the end of the year. There are many ways of completing this journey.

Children live up to the challenges set for them. If the challenges are high and students are encouraged to take risks and supported along the way, then they tend to surprise us with what they can accomplish. Students are eager to please and showcase what they know and what they can do.

Establishing strong rapport with students helps build their confidence and encourages them to stretch beyond what they thought possible.

Building rapport with students also helps develop character strength—the soft skills not present in subject curricula. Students want to achieve. They want to get better at doing things. If you recognize this within your students, make connections with them, and let them know they are safe and supported, then they will look up to you, admire you, and remember you as the person who believed in them. It is you they will acknowledge as helping to foster a skill or passion.

Students need leadership. They need guidance. They need influential adults.

How do you build rapport with students?

1. Describe your ideal student. What is the student's academic attitude? What is the student's behavior? How does the student interact with his classmates? How does the student respond to her teachers?
2. How do you motivate students to engage them in the lesson?
3. How do you build strong rapport with students?
4. **Scenario**: You notice that a student has lost interest entirely in your subject. She is not completing homework or participating in class. What do you do?
5. **Scenario**: You learn that you will be getting a student in your class that has a reputation for being difficult. What do you do to ensure the student transitions into your class effectively and achieves success?

Series 11: Role of Parents

Effective teachers recognize the role parents play in their child's education and leverage this position to achieve their curriculum goals. Parents are significant stakeholders. Finding ways to get them involved with their child's learning means you increase your influence, meet your curriculum expectations, and build your credibility as an effective educator.

In the very early years, parents want to see their child developing well, adjusting to new environments, and achieving success at each milestone. When the child enters elementary school, parents are eager to see him transition into a successful learner. Parents might find themselves supporting the teacher by helping their child learn to read or write or practice math drills. At this stage, it can be easy and gratifying to be a part of their child's learning.

Once the child has a foundation in reading and writing and has developed good learning skills, the child is more than capable of success without so much parental involvement. By this point, many parents will have left the education of their child to the teachers as the experts. Other parents, eager for success beyond a particular level, will remain quite involved right through to university entrance.

When you consider the role of parents in education, invariably, they want what is best for their children. They want their children to have all the opportunities and advantages that others have. They want their children to be liked and respected by their teachers and their classmates. They want reassurance that their children are progressing well, that they are challenged to learn, and treated fairly.

As with students, building rapport with parents increases trust.

How do you go about building rapport with parents? How do you convince the committee that this is important to you and to the success of your students?

1. What do you consider to be the role of parents in a child's education?
2. How do you build rapport with parents?
3. Given your experiences, have you had opportunities to interact with the parents of your students? If so, what worked for you?
4. How can parents support what you are doing in the classroom?
5. How do you ensure appropriate lines of communication are maintained?
6. What forms of communication do you maintain with parents? How frequently? How does this help you achieve your goal?
7. **Scenario:** A parent calls you to complain about a test result. How do you respond?
8. **Scenario:** A parent calls the principal to complain about your teaching style. What do you do?

Series 12: School Community

Schools are communities filled with various people functioning in a variety of roles. Within the school, there are professionals in a host of disciplines: teachers, teacher-assistants, support staff, vice principals and principals, learning resource specialists, therapists, nurses, cooking staff, cleaning staff, athletic coaches, music instructors, drama leaders, and on and on. In addition, parents are involved in their child's schooling by helping out in the classroom, volunteering on committees, running fundraising events, attending sporting competitions, musicals, speaking events, and on.

Your reputation and your influence are far-reaching. Most students will know you or have heard of you—if they have not had you as a teacher. They will have an impression of what you are like, whether you are tough, or funny, or kind. Parents will know you far better and spend hours discussing you in parking lots, coffee shops, or birthday parties. They have highly forged impressions of you built through repetitions of the same messages they have heard from other parents, parents whose children are currently in your class or whose children were formerly your students.

You might never know how much time parents will have spent thinking about you, hoping or fearing that you will be their child's teacher, anticipating the best or the worst.

At times, your colleagues, vice principals, and principals will also hear about you either directly or indirectly from parents or students, and your reputation will continue to build. You will be praised or chastised. Your reputation will pervade the minds of the community, and all your behaviors and actions will be judged accordingly.

Fortunately, teachers are far too busy with their own responsibilities— meeting standards, the needs of the school, and their students—to give reputation much attention.

The purpose of the above scenario isn't to scare teachers from pursuing this profession—nor is it to insult parents who only want the best for their children—but it is to describe what a typical school community is like. Understanding this allows a prospective candidate to prepare more effectively.

The panel needs to choose a teacher who possesses all of the great qualities of an effective educator. But *fitting in* the school community is critical. How will students perceive you? How will your colleagues perceive you? How will parents perceive you? Each is an important question that needs answering.

1. What does school community mean to you?
2. What role do teachers play in a school community?
3. What steps would you take to immerse yourself in this school community?
4. How do you see yourself contributing to the school culture?
5. In what ways can you contribute to the school community outside the classroom?
6. What experiences have you had with leading extracurricular or cocurricular programs?

Series 13: Personality Traits

When you consider that every other applicant will have had a somewhat similar amount of prior education in their undergraduate program and in their postgraduate certification program, you realize that schools are not really looking for someone who has had a unique teacher certification background. After all, programs are much the same across the country. The great differentiator is not in education but in personality.

This is ultimately what a panel is looking for: a person who is engaging and can motivate students to learn; someone who challenges herself and her students, setting high standards for each; someone who can take risks in her teaching, be flexible, adapt to change, and improve upon her performance; someone who has integrity and treats students with fairness and respect; and someone who demands excellence in her own performance and models excellence for students. This educator is self-confident, thorough, decisive, a pleasure to be around. She thinks about what is best for the students and figures out ways for them to learn, experiment, and grow. She serves as a model to others on staff, who watch her with admiration because of her caring and drive. Ultimately, this is what an interview panel is looking for.

Schools have their own internal set of mission statements, vision statements, goals, institutional memory, and cultural identity. Being a member of a faculty is being a member of a team. Senior teachers have already learned and adapted to the school culture. They have embraced its values and philosophy and exercise these in all that they do. Interviewing committees are looking for someone who can easily integrate with this established environment. They are looking for someone who is going to absorb the culture, adapt where necessary, and enrich the school.

Personality questions might be explicitly asked—panelists want to know what your dominant characteristics are. Or they might be implied—embedded throughout the interview.

Each of the following interview questions tackles personality traits from differing perspectives.

1. What personal character traits make you an effective teacher?
2. What would you consider to be your greatest attributes and how do you see them adding to your success as an educator?
3. What three adjectives would best describe you?
4. How would your colleagues describe you?
5. What would your students say about you?
6. How would your previous employers describe you?
7. What would you say are your strongest work habits?

Series 14: Interpersonal Skills

At its very core, teaching is about working with people. In any school setting, teachers work closely with three constituent groups: students, colleagues, and administrators. Depending on how community oriented the school is, teachers might also interact extensively with parents, external support professionals, colleagues in other schools, board members, local organizations, and the greater school community.

The education profession needs teachers that are personable, approachable, and compassionate. Teachers must have excellent people skills. Students require empathy and understanding and need to feel comfortable around their teachers. Teachers must work closely with others in team-teaching initiatives, in planning and assessing, and in professional development activities. In this way, employers are looking for cooperative, supportive, resourceful, and engaging people. Teachers can also be called on to work closely with parents, especially in the early years or in school communities where parents are encouraged to participate in many aspects of school life.

Having strong people skills is a necessity in this profession. An educator must have an engaging personality. She must be effective at influencing others, especially her students. She must be a team player, at times leading and always contributing. Building relationships and developing rapport with all constituents is key.

But given the demands of teaching, educators frequently find themselves as silos in their own classroom, so wrapped up in the daily business of teaching that they lose out on opportunities to interact with colleagues except in the staffroom or during cocurricular responsibilities. There is a danger of becoming too isolated and removed from the school culture. How do you ensure you balance the needs of your classroom with the needs of the school?

There are thousands and thousands of schools, each with its own cultural milieu. Some schools encourage independence and innovation driven by individuals in their own classrooms. Other schools foster collaboration and collegiality motivated by group dynamics and the school as a collective. Just as there are many different types of learners, there are many different types of teachers. Both types are needed.

Series 4 questions are about your individual personality. Series 11 questions are about your group skills. The former is about what makes you effective as an individual teacher, the latter about your effectiveness in a group setting. Differentiating between the two types of questions being asked in an interview is instructive. If you find that questions are predominantly about your ability to interact with others and work closely in collaborative circles, then you know the school favors this approach and you can better determine whether this is the right place for you. On the other hand, if you find that the questions favor independence, it is more likely that the school acknowledges its faculty as specialists in their own disciplines and working in isolation in their own classrooms. In this scenario, the school expects less interaction from its faculty.

Which is the right place for you? Both types of schools are needed, as are both types of people. Which are you?

1. What is your working relationship with your principals and vice principals?
2. What is your working relationship with your teacher-colleagues?
3. Have you team-taught before? What was your team-teaching experience like?
4. How do you feel about working closely with colleagues in a team-teaching situation? How do you feel about sharing your planning?
5. **Example:** Describe an experience you have had in which you have collaborated with a team. What did you find helpful in that experience?
6. **Example:** Describe an experience in which you have disagreed with the leadership of the school. How did you handle it?

Series 15: Communication Skills

Effective communication in oral and written form means students understand what is expected of them. Ineffective communication leads to confusion, misunderstanding, and a poor performance in learning and behavior. Effective communicators use clear and precise language. They convince and persuade.

As an educator, you teach lessons, assign tasks, manage behavior, praise accomplishments, and give feedback. You write instructions, comments, and report cards. You make phone calls, generate e-mails, and record videos. There are so many opportunities to communicate.

An interview committee wants to know that you are an effective communicator. They want assurance that students will not be confused by what you say or how you say it. They want certainty that parents will understand and respect you.

For the most part, the screening phone call will have given the committee members an indication of your effectiveness as a communicator. The interview helps confirm their suspicions. The panelists are also looking to determine which methods you most often use and how frequently you communicate. Keeping samples of work in your portfolio helps.

1. What form of communication do you maintain with parents?
2. What mediums of communication do you use in your classroom?

3. Do you have samples of lesson plans?
4. Do you have samples of report card comments?

Series 16: Communication Technology and Social Media

You will most likely find computers in virtually every grade and subject, as they have become increasingly more accessible and inexpensive. Leveraging technology and social media to advance learning is important. Some schools embrace these and want to be on the leading edge; others are very conservative in nature. The spectrum is vast. Knowing the school's tech initiatives will help greatly.

In any case, there are many ways to enhance education through technology and social media. Continuing to embrace new mediums and incorporate a few in your practice will help you improve as an educator. Some programs take a while to learn and teach, with results indicating little direct correlation with student success. This is a waste of time for you and for the students. Other programs are easy to learn and use and are very effective at producing results. Being a discerning user of technology and social media helps with screening which are best to use and which will produce positive outcomes.

There is a lot of mixed emotion when it comes to discussing technology. Schools that can afford the latest hardware and software give teachers a reason to experiment with what works and what doesn't in the classroom. Other schools whose budgets are limited find it difficult to keep abreast of new practices with communication technology. Innovative practitioners who like the first environment will struggle with the second if those interests cannot be met.

1. What role does communication technology play in the classroom?
2. What computer technology skills do you have?
3. How have you used computers effectively in the classroom?
4. What programs are you familiar with and comfortable using to teach?
5. What role does social media play in the classroom? How do you make effective use of it?

Series 17: Personal Interests

Your personal interests are important to you but also to the school. Administrators are interested in who you are as a person and not just as an educator. Your interests reveal your values. Are you musical, athletic, dramatic? Do you enjoy arts and crafts? Do you devote time to social causes? Do you enjoy activity, reading, learning? And on and on.

Frequently, committees are looking for teachers who can enhance their school further. Running a club, leading a team, conducting a band are potential opportunities to contribute to the school community beyond the classroom.

This is a great opportunity to leverage your outside interests in order to secure the position. Preparing some responses in which you showcase your talents and skills in a way that enhances the school brings you much closer to the contract. Obviously, school-related interests are always required: guitar club, coaching basketball, Model United Nations club. But many passions can be converted to clubs or teams.

A young teacher is passionate about making her own jewelry. She pitches it to the principal, secures a budget, and now runs a jewelry-making club. Another, a SCUBA instructor on the side, brings this to the attention of the interviewing panel, and now the school yearly runs a marine biology trip in which biology students spend a week investigating a coral reef. A third finds the need to address the HIV-AIDS epidemic in her school and begins a social awareness campaign and generates immense financial support for the organization. The options are endless and often don't require financial resources. Sometimes all that is needed is a proposal of what you can do to engage students in a nonclassroom environment.

Committees are drawn to candidates like these. After all, what are you really doing? Building rapport with the students? Engaging them in experiential learning? Giving of your time to support a worthy cause? These are all characteristics desired by administrators.

1. What do you do in your spare time?
2. What interests do you have outside of education?
3. What are your personal interests?
4. What can you do to enhance the school community?

5. What do you see yourself doing five years from now?

6. How do you see yourself contributing to the long-term growth and success of this school?

Series 18: Questions for the Interview Panel

The final series of questions are yours. After so many questions from the panelists, it is your turn. Don't pass up the opportunity.

The kinds of questions to ask are not those that reveal you don't know much about their school—after all, if you have done your research correctly, you should know a lot already. One effective strategy is to use a piece of information you know about the school in the form of a question, allowing the committee then to elaborate on this. For instance, if you are familiar with the school's strategic plan, asking a question about a particular initiative that genuinely interests you reveals multiple things to the committee: you have done your research; this initiative is of personal interest to you; and maybe you can support or champion it. Your curiosity and interest may complement or enhance what the committee has already gathered about you.

You have the opportunity to ask only one or two questions before the interview is finished. Make your questions count.

1. Do you have any questions for us?

Next Steps

What do you do now? Where do you go from here? How many times have you practiced your responses? How polished are they? Can you take an interview at a moment's notice without having to review any further?

Conclusion

Now What?

Although you have done much to prepare yourself for a teaching position, the job search process doesn't end at this point. There is a lot you can still do to enhance yourself as a worthy prospect. Consider each of the following areas as opportunities to increase your exposure, your breadth of understanding of the teaching profession, and your marketability as an educator.

What to Do While Waiting for That Teaching Position

In your search for the ideal teaching position, time is on your side. Rather than rushing in blindly to pursue the first teaching position that you see advertised, act strategically and focus your energy on achieving that desired dream job. As you do so, take the time to work on the following:

1. **Build Your Network.** Make contacts with everyone in the field of education: teachers, specialists, vice principals, principals, and professors. Get their contact information. Share your passion with them and your desire to teach. Talk to them about your hopes as an educator, your ideal classroom, and the work you have done to prepare for the teaching position and for the interview. Impress them. They are your direct line to a job.

2. **Develop Your Marketability.** Make yourself more desirable as an educator. What can you do to broaden your appeal? At this point in your career, you are selling yourself. Administrators will

pay for value. How can you show that you are the best value out there?

3. **Immerse Yourself in Your College.** Teachers are professionals backed by a credible set of standards from their college. Read all the literature of your college, make connections with its members, participate in activities, become an active member yourself.

4. **Attend Workshops and Seminars.** Consider diversifying your interests and learning some concepts or skills that will increase your knowledge base and skill set. Attend curricular-related events (teaching, learning, or assessment) or cocurricular events (coaching a team or running a club). Get outside of your comfort zone and try something new. Teachers who are continual learners, who take risks and challenge themselves, serve as excellent role models for students who are doing this on a daily basis.

5. **Take Courses.** Consider acquiring additional qualifications. Take courses that allow you to increase your teachables or further specialize in your discipline. As in the above point, you want to reveal two specific traits: a lifelong love of learning and the need to continually upgrade your credentials.

6. **Read Education Texts.** The Association for Supervision and Curriculum Development (ASCD) is the preeminent education organization, boasting hundreds of education titles on a wide variety of topics. This is a great place to learn about many education concepts as well as master a few. No educator can doubt the value of this treasure chest of great resources.

7. **Watch Education Talks.** There are many current educators giving talks on TED or YouTube on education topics, the state of education, children, and schools. Watching education talks is a great way to complement the writings of the authors.

8. **Increase Your Educator Vocabulary.** Continue to add key education terminology to your vocabulary. Your goal is to maximize your scope of education concepts so that you are well equipped for when the interview takes place or when you begin your first day of teaching.

9. **Practice Your Craft.** Get into a classroom. Volunteer your time. Work closely in the grade and with the subjects you want to teach. Hone your skills. These opportunities give you direct connections with people that will get you hired.

10. **Study Your Discipline.** If you want to become a generalist teaching multiple subjects, you might need to brush up on subjects that you have not studied in a while. If you want to become a specialist teaching one particular subject in higher levels, you can review concepts and begin to plan what you will teach. In each case, you are preparing yourself for the first year of teaching, which will ease your transition to that school and position.

11. **Tutor a Student.** Working one-on-one with individual students is an ideal way to hone your craft. The more time you can spend with a student understanding his learning idiosyncrasies, the more you can develop strategies to appeal to that student's learning style. The more often you can repeat this process with diverse learners, the more strategies you can develop and the more effective you can become as an educator.

12. **Volunteer in a Community Initiative.** There is nothing like getting out of yourself and witnessing life from another person's perspective to give you greater context in your own life. Teachers serve. Get into the volunteer service industry and you will gain a greater appreciation for people and the profession of teaching. There are many social services in need.

13. **Work at a Camp.** Camps are fun and exciting. They are great ways to take on education from a love-of-learning perspective. It is easy to motivate students when activities are fun. You will also be able to practice classroom management and discipline strategies in the less formal setting.

14. **Work on Your Social Media Persona.** Continue to build your professional persona, grow your contacts, and increase your exposure. Develop your professional portfolio.

Final Thoughts

If you have come this far in preparing to teach, then you have positioned yourself well for success. Great teachers are always in need. Keep the three messages presented at the beginning of this book top of mind as you continue to pursue this profession:

- You are a unique individual whose upbringing, educational background, and life experiences have given you distinct values, beliefs, attitudes, and skills;
- You can become the effective educator you want to be and live a fulfilling life teaching students the subjects and grades you desire; and
- You can position yourself well and achieve that teaching job through the right presentation and promotion of your talents.

You will get the job and become the successful educator you want to become. You will have tremendous influence on your students, and they will remember you as one of the most significant teachers in their lives.

Congratulations on becoming a teacher and all the best with your continued success.

Appendix A: Comprehensive List of Interview Questions

Series 1: Introductory Questions and Recent History

1. Tell us a bit about yourself.
2. What are you currently doing? How does this help you in your goal to become a teacher?
3. Why do you want to teach?
4. Why is teaching rewarding for you?
5. Have you had teaching experience before? As a student? As a teacher? Or substitute?

Series 2: Educational Experience

1. Why did you decide to pursue your undergraduate degree?
2. What did you find most rewarding about your undergraduate experiences?
3. Why did you decide not to continue pursuing that field and get a career in that industry?
4. Why did you choose to attend that university for your undergraduate degree?
5. Why did you choose to attend that university for your teacher's college certification?
6. Tell me about your favorite subjects while in teacher's college.

7. What activities did you take part in outside of your academic studies? (athletics, arts, service)
8. Why did you decide to major in preschool, primary, junior, intermediate, or senior education?

Series 3: Teaching and Practicum Experience

1. Describe your student teaching experiences.
2. What was most rewarding about your experiences?
3. What was your greatest challenge? How did you resolve it?
4. What was your working relationship with the associate teacher?
5. How did the students receive and respond to you?
6. How involved were you in communicating with parents?
7. Were you given complete independence in your practicum?
8. How did you go about planning lessons and units?
9. How did you assess and evaluate student performance?
10. What did you learn most from this experience?

Series 4: Philosophy of Teaching

1. Why do you want to teach?
2. Why do you think you would make an effective teacher?
3. What do you find rewarding or fulfilling about teaching?
4. What is your philosophy of teaching?
5. What is your preferred grade level? Discipline? Why?
6. Describe your ideal student.
7. How would you design your classroom? Why?

Series 5: Teaching and Learning

1. How do you keep current?
2. How do you innovate your practice and appeal to the changing needs of the students?
3. What teaching strategies do you employ in your daily lessons?
4. How do you ensure students have learned the material, or the skill, or completed the task properly?

5. How do you individualize instruction?
6. How do you differentiate instruction to meet the needs of the remedial student, the general student, and the enriched student?
7. How do you meet the needs of English language learners?
8. How do you meet the needs of students with differing learning abilities?
9. **Example:** Provide an example in which you remediated a student's learning. Was the process successful? How do you know?
10. **Example:** Provide an example in which you enriched a student's learning. How did you go about designing your plan? What did you learn from the experience?

Series 6: Curriculum Knowledge and Planning

1. How familiar are you with the curriculum guides for your preferred grade or subject?
2. What process do you follow when planning a lesson or unit? Is there a particular model that you have found effective?
3. When planning a lesson or unit, what do you take into consideration?
4. **Example:** Provide one successful lesson you planned. What steps did you take? How do you know you were successful in your planning? What are the indicators?
5. **Example:** Describe one lesson that did not go as well as you intended. What did not seem to work? How did you recover the lesson and ensure there was some success?

Series 7: Assessment and Evaluation

1. What do you believe the purpose of assessment and evaluation to be?
2. What forms of assessment would you use in a given subject and grade?
3. What types of diagnostic, formative, and summative assessment do you like to use? Why?

4. What kinds of assessments do you find most effective? Why?

5. What role do you see self-assessment and self-evaluation playing in student learning?

Series 8: Learning Environment

1. If you had the opportunity to design your ideal classroom, what would the physical space look like? Paint a picture for us of what we would see when walking into your classroom.

2. What furniture would you have in your classroom? How would it be laid out? Why?

3. What would appear on the walls?

4. What kind of atmosphere would you engender in this ideal learning environment?

5. If we walked into your classroom, what would we see students doing? How would we see them behaving?

Series 9: Classroom Management

1. How do you establish order and process in your classroom?

2. What strategies have you found effective in managing a classroom?

3. What techniques have you found effective in handling discipline?

4. **Scenario:** Two boys have been repeatedly fighting in your classroom and while you have kindly asked them to stop, this behavior continues. What do you do?

5. **Scenario:** A student continues to challenge your authority in the class and while you have asked her nicely to stop, she insists on making it difficult for you. How do you handle the situation?

Series 10: Students

1. Describe your ideal student. What is the student's academic attitude? What is the student's behavior? How does the student interact with his classmates? How does the student respond to her teachers?

2. How do you motivate students to engage them in the lesson?
3. How do you build a strong rapport with students?
4. **Scenario:** You notice that a student has lost interest entirely in your subject. She isn't completing homework, participating in class. What do you do?
5. **Scenario:** You learn that you'll be getting a student in your class that has a reputation for being difficult. What do you do to ensure the student transitions into your class effectively and achieves success?

Series 11: Role of Parents

1. What do you consider to be the role of parents in the child's education?
2. How do you build rapport with parents?
3. Given your experiences, have you had opportunities to interact with parents of your students? If so, what worked for you?
4. How can parents support what you're doing in the classroom?
5. How do you ensure appropriate lines of communication are maintained?
6. What forms of communication do you maintain with parents? How frequently? How does this help you achieve your goal?
7. **Scenario:** A parent calls you to complain about a test result. How do you respond?
8. **Scenario:** A parent calls the principal to complain about your teaching style. What do you do?

Series 12: School Community

1. What does school community mean to you?
2. What role do teachers play in a school community?
3. What steps would you take to immerse yourself in this school community?
4. How do you see yourself contributing to the school culture?
5. In what ways can you contribute to the school community outside the classroom?

6. What experiences have you had with leading extracurricular or cocurricular programs?

Series 13: Personality Traits

1. What personal character traits make you an effective teacher?
2. What would you consider to be your greatest attributes and how do you see them adding to your success as an educator?
3. What three adjectives would best describe you?
4. How would your colleagues describe you?
5. What would your students say about you?
6. How would your previous employers describe you?
7. What would you say are your strongest work habits?

Series 14: Interpersonal Skills

1. What is your working relationship with your principals and vice principals?
2. What is your working relationship with your teacher-colleagues?
3. Have you team-taught before? What was your team-teaching experience like?
4. How do you feel about working closely with colleagues in a team-teaching situation? How do you feel about sharing your planning?
5. **Example:** Describe an experience you have had in which you have collaborated with a team. What did you find helpful in that experience?
6. **Example:** Describe an experience in which you have disagreed with the leadership of the school or business. How did you handle it?

Series 15: Communication Skills

1. What form of communication do you maintain with parents?
2. What mediums of communication do you use in your classroom?
3. Do you have samples of lesson plans?

4. Do you have samples of report card comments?

Series 16: Communication Technology and Social Media

1. What role does communication technology play in the classroom?
2. What computer technology skills do you have?
3. How have you used computers effectively in the classroom?
4. What programs are you familiar with and comfortable using to teach?
5. What role does social media play in the classroom? How do you make effective use of it?

Series 17: Personal Interests

1. What do you do in your spare time?
2. What interests do you have outside of education?
3. What are your personal interests?
4. What can you do to enhance the school community?
5. What do you see yourself doing five years from now?
6. How do you see yourself contributing to the long-term growth and success of this school?

Series 18: Questions for the Interview Panel

1. Do you have any questions for us?

Appendix B—
Becoming a Better Teacher

Self-Reflective Practice

Teaching is a very dynamic process: education theories change, student knowledge and skill sets change, subject matter changes. Education provides many opportunities for mastering your craft. No matter how many years you'll serve as a teacher, there'll always be something new that you'll need to embrace. This could be a new theory, a new process, a new technology, or even a student whose learning style you have not encountered yet. Leaving yourself flexible to change is vital to your success as an educator.

Annually reflecting on your teaching practice is a great way to remain fresh, review your own performance, and set goals for the coming year.

As well, this is an effective strategy to complete following each of your practicums, long-term occasional placements, and volunteer experiences.

General Goals

1. Have I achieved the goals I set for myself?

Curriculum Knowledge and Planning

2. Have I demonstrated complete competence in the subject matter I teach? Where do I need to review concepts to improve my practice for the next time I teach this subject?
3. Have I planned my lessons and units using a variety of teaching strategies and approaches?
4. Have I appealed to multiple intelligences in my planning? Have I appealed to different learning styles?

Assessment and Evaluation

5. Have I varied the types of assessments I offer? Have I included a broad range in which some target specific expectations and others—rich performance tasks—target many expectations?
6. Have I designed assessments that appeal to many and varied learning styles?
7. Have I used peer and self-evaluation effectively?

School Standards / Academic Standards

8. Have I set high standards for student achievement so that they can stretch in their learning?
9. Have I delivered a challenging and rigorous curriculum consistent with student ability levels?

Learning Environment

10. Have I created a safe and supportive environment where students feel comfortable to take risks with their learning without feeling intimidated by others or the task?
11. Have I designed the layout of the classroom well? Do I have a variety of instructional materials posted? Do I have a variety of representative student work posted around the classroom?

Addressing Student Needs

12. Have I appealed to the needs of the students, ensuring that I have addressed their particular learning abilities or circumstances in order to give them the best possible opportunity for success?
13. Have I modeled the role of a lifelong learner (dedication, persistence, self-discipline, passion, focus, and self-confidence)?
14. Have I recognized student achievement and celebrated student successes? Have I encouraged positive learning and reinforced student motivation to learn?

Employing Multiple Teaching Strategies

15. Have I employed various teaching strategies to ensure that all types of learners have had an equal advantage to learn?
16. Have I integrated various media?

Building Community

17. Have I built rapport with each student?
18. Have I developed rapport with parents? Have I increased their comfort and confidence in me as an educator who is addressing their child's best interests?
19. Have I developed a strong relationship among the team members in my department or division? Have I shared in responsibilities and given of my skills to others in the department?

Practicing Professionalism

20. Have I practiced the standards of professionalism in all my conduct with student, colleagues, parents, and administrators?
21. Have I employed diplomacy when necessary and ensured a win-win situation between parties?
22. Have I done what is in the best interests of the students?
23. Have my evaluations of student learning been fair?

Managing the Classroom

24. Have I practiced discipline strategies that leave students with dignity?
25. Have I provided opportunities for students to resolve conflict in mutually respectful manners?

Leadership

26. Have I demonstrated leadership in all my actions and activities?

Communication

27. Have I been clear in my communication with students?
28. Have I been frequent and thoughtful in my communication with parents?

Providing Additional Attention

29. Have I addressed student needs beyond the classroom?

Professional Development

30. Have I attended professional development opportunities including in-service, workshops, conferences, and courses and applied these to my practice?
31. Have I developed and offered my own workshop?

Service

32. Have I modeled the value of good citizenship by giving back to the community? In what ways have I demonstrated this? How can I demonstrate this further?

Final Thought

33. Have I been effective?

References

Ainsworth, Paul. *Get That Teaching Job!* New York: Continuum Internation Publication Group, 2012.

Bolles, Richard N. *What Color Is Your Parachute? A Practical Manual for Job-Hunters and Career-Changers.* New York: Crown Publishing Group, 2012.

Canter, Lee, and Marlene Canter. *Assertive Discipline: Positive Behavior Management for Today's Classroom.* Santa Monica: Lee Canter & Associates, 1992.

———. *Succeeding with Difficult Students: New Strategies for Reaching Your Most Challenging Students.* Santa Monica: Lee Canter & Associates, 1993.

Coloroso, Barbara. *kids are worth it!* New York: Harper Collins, 2010.

———. *The Bully, the Bullied, and the Bystander.* New York: Harper Collins, 2010.

Covey, Stephen R. *Principle-Centered Leadership.* New York: Free Press, 1991.

———. *The Seven Habits of Highly Effective People.* New York: Simon and Schuster, 1989.

Demartini, John. *The Values Factor: The Secret to Creating an Inspired and Fulfilling Life.* New York: the Berkley Publishing Group, 2013.

Enelow, Wendy S. *Expert Resumes for Teachers and Educators.* Indianapolis: JIST Inc, 2011.

Fredericks, Anthony D. *Ace Your Teacher Interview: 149 Fantastic Answers to Tough Questions.* St. Paul: JIST Works, 2012.

Gisler, Margaret. *101 Career Alternatives for Teachers: Exciting Job Opportunities for Teachers Outside the Profession.* Roseville: Prima Pub, 2002.

Grensing-Pophal, Lin. *The Everything Resume Book: From Using Social Media to Choosing the Right Keywords, All You Need to Have A Resume That Stands Out From the Crowd!* Avon: Adams Media, 2013.

Heller, Daniel A. *Teachers Wanted: Attracting and Retaining Good Teachers.* Alexandria: Association for Supervision and Curriculum Development (ASCCD), 2004.

Hindman, Jennifer L., and James H. Stronge. *The Teacher Quality Index: A Protocol for Teacher Selection.* Alexandria: Association for Supervision and Curriculum Development, 2006.

Hindman, Jennifer L., James H. Stronge, and Pamela D. Tucker. *Handbook for Qualities of Effective Teachers.* Alexandria: Association for Supervision and Curriculum Development, 2004.

Lacy, Kyle, and Erik Deckers. *Branding Yourself: How to Use Social Media to Invent or Reinvent Yourself.* New York: Pearson Education Inc., 2013.

Littky, Dennis. *The Big Picture: Education Is Everyone's Business.* Alexandria: Association for Supervision and Curriculum Development, 2004.

McKay, Dawn Rosenberg. *The Everything Practice Interview Book: Make the Best Impression—and Get the Job You Want*. Avon: Adams Media, 2009.

McKinney, Anne. *Real-Resumes for Teachers*. Fayetteville: Prep Publications, 2000.

Robinson, Ken. *The Element: How Finding Your Passion Changes Everything*. New York: Penguin Group, 2009.

Seligman, Martin E. P. *Authentic Happiness: Using the New Positive Psychology to Realize Your Potential for Lasting Fulfillment*. New York: Free Press, 2002.

———. *Flourish: A Visionary New Understanding of Happiness and Well-being*. New York: Atria Paperback, 2011.

Sherer, Marge. *A Better Beginning: Supporting and Mentoring New Teachers*. Alexandria: Association for Supervision and Curriculum Development, 1999.

Wagner, Tony. *Creating Innovators: The Making of Young People Who Will Change the World*. New York: Scribner, 2012.

———. *The Global Achievement Gap: Why Even Our Best Schools Don't Teach the New Survival Skills Our Children Need—and What We Can Do about It*. New York: Perseus Books Group, 2008.

Warner, Jack. *Inside Secrets of Finding a Teaching Job: The Most Effective Search Methods for Both New and Experienced Educators*. Indianapolis: JIST Works, 2006.

Wiggins, Grant, and Jay McTighe. *Essential Questions*. Alexandria: Association for Supervision and Curriculum Development, 2013.

Wiggins, Grant, and Jay McTighe. *Understanding by Design*. Alexandria: Association for Supervision and Curriculum Development, 2005.

About the Author

Carlos Heleno is an educator with more than twenty years of teaching and administrative experience. Since receiving his master's of science in education from Niagara University, he has worked extensively with students, faculty, and administrators to plan, create, and deliver rigorous academic programs. He speaks regularly to new faculty about what it takes to get hired and coaches teachers through the application and interview process.

Index

Printed in the United States
By Bookmasters